3

Patterns of Generosity in America

A Twentieth Century Fund Paper

PATTERNS *of* GENEROSITY IN AMERICA

Who's Holding the Safety Net?

Julian Wolpert

1993 • The Twentieth Century Fund Press • New York

The Twentieth Century Fund sponsors and supervises timely analyses of economic policy, foreign affairs, and domestic political issues. Not-for-profit and nonpartisan, the Fund was founded in 1919 and endowed by Edward A. Filene.

Library of Congress Cataloging-in-Publication Data

Wolpert, Julian
    Patterns of generosity in America: who's holding the safety net? / Julian Wolpert.
       p. cm.
    "A Twentieth Century Fund paper."
    Includes bibliographical references and index.
    ISBN 0–87078–183–9 : $9.95
  1. United States--Social policy--1993-   2. Human services--United States--Finance.   3. Decentralization in government--United States.
4. Intergovernmental fiscal relations--United States.   5. Charities--United States.   6. Quality of life--United States.   7. Social values--United States.   I. Title.
HN59.2.W65   1993
361.6'1'0973--dc20   93-27777
                                            CIP

Cover Design and Illustration: Claude Goodwin
Manufactured in the United States of America.

Foreword

A history of special economic good fortune has spared America many of the explicit political struggles over income distribution and social welfare. We tax our people, compared to other modern industrialized nations, at relatively low levels, and we tolerate a greater imbalance in wealth than do virtually all of our democratic counterparts. Episodes like the Great Depression and initiatives like the Great Society certainly resulted in major leaps forward in the area of social legislation; but, at heart, the American approach to poverty is through the marketplace. For those temporarily left behind, we favor private charity over government dole. Even the stagnant growth in workers' wages over the last twenty years has not led to a sweeping reappraisal of the social contract.

None of this means, of course, that the United States is not home to millions of poor people. Indeed, in the last decade or so, we have gone backward in reducing the number of citizens who live below the poverty line. Over the same period, we also reduced many, if not most, federal programs targeted at assisting low income groups. It is not difficult to explain why.

In the main, the men and women who came to Washington with Ronald Reagan were convinced that taxes were too high and that government was too large. They were consistent in averring that almost any task could be performed better and more efficiently by the private sector. These concepts underpinned a broad range of policy choices for the administration. They were the foundation of a systematic effort to influence the American people in their thinking and approach to a host of issues.

In the area of social policy, the Reagan administration maintained that then current federal levels and mechanisms for supporting the needy were wasteful and counterproductive. This overexpenditure was redressed by significant reductions in federal spending on certain social programs coupled with a call, especially during the "kinder, gentler"

Bush years, for voluntary efforts to offset any harm done to the truly needy. The notion was that America's unique commitment to philanthropy and personal giving (both of time and money) would protect those who were genuinely deserving but who had lost out during the necessary elimination of traditional imprudent federal programs. In addition, the language of those advocating these changes often referred to the states and, to a lesser extent, localities as institutions more in touch with real needs and possibly ready to restore the safety net for those less fortunate through no fault of their own.

While numerous studies have been made of the impact of the Reagan–Bush cuts and of state and local reactions, there is no comprehensive examination of the charitable sector's response to the reductions in national programs and to the exhortations to assist those innocent bystanders hurt by the changes. In an effort to help fill this gap in understanding and research, the Twentieth Century Fund supported this work by Professor Julian Wolpert of Princeton University. He brings special credentials to the task. As a Henry G. Bryant Professor of Geography, Public Affairs and Urban Planning at the Woodrow Wilson School of Public and International Affairs and director of its Program in Urban and Regional Planning, Wolpert has done extensive research—both quantitative and qualitative—into the related issues of philanthropy, government spending, and the nonprofit sector.

The Twentieth Century Fund has a longstanding interest in issues of government spending and social services. It has just commissioned a study from Theda Skocpol on how American social policy treats the old and the young. Also under way is a study of the fiscal crisis and American federalism by Paul Peterson. And Robert Haveman is examining the tendency of Americans to allocate resources for short-term solutions at the expense of the future.

We thank Julian Wolpert for his efforts. Perhaps in some measure they will help move the debate over social policy away from the myth that, when it comes to poverty, government is the problem, and lead us back to a balanced assessment of the ways in which it can be part of the solution. More generally, if we do not learn to think of those activities we carry out on a shared basis—government preeminent among them—as worthwhile, we shall continue to find that the quality of our communities and of our lives is failing to improve, however much we achieve the state of the art in our marketplaces.

Richard C. Leone, *President*
The Twentieth Century Fund
November 1993

Contents

Preface

During the 1980s, virtually all nations were attracted to the potential benefits of decentralizing government domestic programs. America's New Federalism gave enhanced responsibility for support of social, educational, and cultural services to state and local governments and nonprofit organizations. A decade later, assessments of this decentralization experiment show mixed and uneven results. Americans differ widely by community and region in levels of wealth and distress, in the fiscal resources of their state and local governments and voluntary organizations, and in their levels of public and private generosity and willingness to provide support for amenities, services, and income transfers. Decentralization has had some highly regressive effects that are difficult to remedy by government or the voluntary sector solely at state and community levels. The evidence warrants selective recentralization to help guarantee nationally adequate safety nets and quality of life.

The research discussed in this paper is part of a larger study being conducted with support from the Twentieth Century Fund and the Nonprofit Research Fund at the Aspen Institute. Portions of this paper were presented at the Association for Research on Nonprofit Organizations and Voluntary Action Annual Conference at the Program on Nonprofit Organizations, Yale University, New Haven, on October 30, 1992, and at the Independent Sector's Research Forum in San Antonio on March 18, 1993.

1.

The Policy Issues

Generosity is the deployment of available resources to assist the needy, improve access to services, and enhance the variety and quality of life. While Americans tend to be a generous people, some places in America are a lot more generous than others. Residents in some states and localities pay a higher rate of taxes to underwrite relatively generous income support and service programs. They may also devote a greater share of income to their schools, public hospitals, and civic and cultural institutions. They enjoy higher service levels than residents in the more parsimonious places. The persistent federalism issue here is the policy response to disparities resulting from unevenness, not just in fiscal resources, but in the generosity of localities.

The classic example of public sector generosity is the Aid to Families with Dependent Children (AFDC) program. Unlike Social Security benefits, which are uniform throughout the United States, states establish their own AFDC benefit levels and terms. The variations among them cannot be accounted for solely by differences in income levels, fiscal resources, and cost of living.[1] Relative generosity is also, and significantly, determined by local history, political culture, and social welfare attitudes. Some states pay less than would seem fiscally affordable or necessary to maintain safety nets; others are quite generous with their state tax revenues.

This paper will show that state-to-state variations in AFDC benefits are not an isolated phenomena, but are symptomatic of more pervasive place-to-place differences in public sector generosity in both state and local governments. The empirical evidence also shows place-to-place variations in private generosity, such as donations to nonprofit organizations that provide social, cultural, health, and educational services.

1

These differences, too, cannot be explained solely by differences in community wealth, cost of living, or levels of distress. Places that are generous in their state and local government programs tend to be generous in their charitable contributions as well.

The equity implications of these community differences are severe. Decentralization—a goal pursued aggressively by the federal government during the 1980s—took a great deal of funding responsibility away from federal sources and gave greater discretion to state and local authorities. Those who rely on social support or services have therefore become more dependent not just on state and local wealth and fiscal resources, but on local values and social preferences. The fundamental policy question becomes how to ensure equity and fairness under these circumstances.

The question over equity has been at the heart of the New Federalism debate. Fortunately, evidence is now becoming available to permit evaluation of many of the federal decentralization efforts. In addition to data on the public sector, recent compilation of data on the nonprofit sector allows us to examine a service delivery system that has become increasingly important but is even more fragmented than government.

The central question posed by this paper is the wisdom of continuing to pursue decentrist policies across the welfare, educational, cultural, and health sectors. In particular, how should responsibility for maintaining safety nets, amenities, and quality of life be shared between units of government at federal, state, and local levels and among charitable institutions? What difference does it make if service responsibility is federally administered at the national level or if financing responsibility and discretion are transferred to state and local governments and to nonprofit organizations? Why do national or decentralized authority and program standards matter, especially at this point in time? This last question is especially relevant now because important lessons from the New Federalism experiments in decentralization and devolution of federal functions undertaken during the Reagan and Bush administrations can inform the current policy options. Integrating nonprofit organizations into the analysis is especially valuable because those institutions were expected to take on added responsibility for service provision according to the Reagan–Bush New Federalism agenda.

Organization of the Paper

This paper begins by defining *generosity* as it applies to both the private and public sectors and tracing the development of the shared responsibility for service support between nonprofit and government

sectors. While generosity is difficult to measure directly, a set of indicators is proposed and can be used comparatively to assess the variations
among metropolitan areas. A model of generosity based on these indicators is proposed and can be used to test the conventional wisdom
that variations from place-to-place in private and public sector generosity can be explained by differences in local resources and levels of
distress. An alternative explanation is proposed and tested: that persistent local and regional differences in political culture and social welfare
values play a significant role in accounting for the service disparities.
The paper concludes by looking at the positive and negative lessons of
decentralization from the 1980s and suggesting policy remedies for
government and nonprofits in terms of retaining a decentralized structure where beneficial and restoring greater national integration where
fragmentation has proven dysfunctional.

2.

Organized Generosity and Its Public and Private Dimensions

T he term *generosity* refers here to a willingness to contribute funds either through public or voluntary sectors. Generosity can be prompted by pure altruism or by mixed motives and enlightened self-interest.[1] Generosity has mixed motives when donors may potentially benefit either directly or indirectly from their contributions. Donors or their families may use the services themselves (for example, attend the concerts performed by the symphony orchestra to which they contribute) or benefit indirectly from the improved health and social well-being in the communities their voluntary contributions and tax dollars help to support. The assumption is made that altruism can account for modest generosity levels, but more substantial giving presumes an expectation of direct or indirect benefits to donors.

Generosity includes both public (that is, governmental) and private support for services and amenities that require supplements or subsidies to make them available at all, or to make them affordable to a wider range of users, or free to those who cannot afford even minimal fees. In contrast, a true gift would imply no opportunity for donor benefit.[2] Charity refers to monetary donations to those least fortunate, while philanthropy generally means substantial support by foundations, corporations, and private donors for nonprofit institutions that provide worthy services or work toward solving significant social problems.[3] The analysis here focuses on the broader concept of generosity rather than gifts and philanthropy because available data do not allow us to identify how services are distributed to beneficiaries.

The Dimensions of Generosity

The evidence that Americans are quite generous is shown by the extensive volunteerism and the $125 billion donated in 1992 to help support the services provided by hundreds of thousands of nonprofit organizations scattered throughout the nation. Americans are also generous in their support for, and willingness to be taxed by, government to finance transfer payments and a variety of social and welfare services. Public sector generosity is reflected by the many federal, state, and local programs that assist low-income, elderly, and handicapped populations with both income supplements and services.

Government programs also support a variety of educational, health, and cultural (that is, amenity) services, only some of which are targeted to low-income populations. Thus, both private and public sector generosity includes a component that is largely *distributive* (support intended to reduce inequality) as well as an *amenity* component (support intended to enhance the variety and quality of life).

Public sector and private generosity are often directly linked. Some localities may contribute very generously to the Salvation Army and the Y and support reduced municipal or state funds for general relief; other places might contribute a smaller share of income directly to voluntary agencies, but support greater public expenditures for day care or housing the homeless. Theory suggests that government expenditures crowd out voluntary contributions and that less government involvement in social support would stimulate private giving. Yet the evidence shows that public and private generosity are more generally complementary.

Major Findings

The primary findings from the empirical research and analysis in this paper include the following:

1. Americans are not uniformly generous but vary significantly from place-to-place in their level and targeting of government and nonprofit sector generosity.

2. Economic inequalities and fiscal disparities between states, local governments, and nonprofit organizations yield highly

uneven support from place-to-place for transfer payments and social services, impacting the lowest-income population most severely.

3. Disparities in generosity levels from place-to-place have been declining, principally due to the harsher economic environment in the more generous places rather than greater generosity in the more parsimonious ones.

4. Places with higher levels of generosity target more of their contributions to nonprofit organizations that provide amenity services (that is, educational, cultural, and health services) than for the more equity-based social services.

5. Support for amenity services is greater where per capita income is increasing, where the political and cultural ideology is liberal, rather than conservative, and in the smaller metropolitan areas where distress levels are lower.

6. Little information is available about beneficiaries of government and nonprofit services, their degree of need, and the population that is not being served.

7. The increased sorting of Americans into socially homogeneous suburban communities has reproduced urban public and nonprofit service infrastructures in the suburbs often at the expense of support for center city and rural institutions. As a result, the real growth of service provision is quite small.

8. Disparities in basic services and quality of life are widening between the states and local metropolitan areas that are growing and those that are in decline.

9. Our severely fragmented and atomized nonprofit sector contributes effectively to the variety and quality of life in American communities but lacks the resources and is not structured to address major service and regional disparities.

3.

Decentralization and Its Limitations

A decade ago, the nation was debating the potential virtues of the New Federalism proposals to decentralize and devolve federal social service programs to state and local governments and non-profit organizations.[1] Decentralization policies were fostered to promote greater efficiency in service provision and to restore a better match between local preferences and willingness to underwrite their costs.[2] The New Federalism was also seen by fiscal conservatives as a mechanism to restrict the growth of federal as well as state and local governments. What was not discussed at the time was that public sector decentralization might discourage generosity and legitimize inequity;[3] rather, local giving and volunteerism were expected to fill the gap left by the federal pullout.

The need to centralize certain welfare and social functions at the national level is substantiated by two concerns: insurance and equity. The insurance issue relates to the benefits of pooling fiscal risks across state and local governments. Since the effects of temporary economic downturns and natural disasters are limited in time and place, a national pool to share the risks ensures every geographical area protection in the face of unexpected hardship or calamity. Americans generally accept the idea that federal aid is needed to assist hurricane victims in Florida, for example, or focus extra resources on areas suffering from military base closings.

The equity argument deals with federal compensation for state and local differences both in fiscal capacity and fiscal effort (that is, generosity) in supporting safety nets and quality of life. The effort dimension is of greatest concern here because inequity arising from profound differences in generosity for distributive programs can seriously undermine the decentrist agenda.

The findings from the decentralization experiment are mixed. The evidence suggests that states, localities, and nonprofits have managed the added responsibility quite efficiently and equitably in some sectors and areas, especially where decentralization was not accompanied by a drastic reduction in federal support. In others, such as welfare, social, income transfer, and general relief, the opposite has occurred. Decentralization and devolution in these generally distributive areas have struck hardest at the lowest-income population.

Left largely to their own preferences and bases of local support, individual states and communities responded very differently. Some places attempted to sustain or even augment programs, while others cut back severely. As a result, disparities in support for social programs widened from place-to-place during the prosperous period of the mid-1980s. However, the economic downturn in the late 1980s and early 1990s perversely reduced the most extreme disparities, primarily through cutbacks by many of the traditionally more generous places. These were hard hit and forced to cut budgets and stiffen eligibility requirements for welfare and related service programs. Fifteen states cut AFDC payments, or tightened eligibility, or both. Seven states cut their general assistance grants that go to support single adults.

The existence of disparities led to concerns among states with relatively generous welfare payments and social programs that they were acting as magnets for attracting low-income people from poorer or more parsimonious states. Persuaded by this argument, legislators in California, the nation's fourth most generous state, have been attempting to cut benefits and limit welfare benefits to newcomers to what they were getting in their home states.

The immediate issue of state welfare policies and the generosity of their programs in boom or bust periods touches upon fundamental concerns that merit reexamination by the new administration in Washington. Should a single national standard of social support and services replace the separate state and local standards (much like Social Security payments, which do not vary from place-to-place)? Should national standards also apply to other public sector programs that are targeted to children, the elderly, or the handicapped population? Furthermore, if a case can be made that income transfers and social services should not discriminate according to place of residence, wouldn't the same argument apply to public support of educational, health, and cultural services?

The disputes over centralized or local control and targeting of the provision of services are symbolic of fundamental conflicts in national and regional political cultures and social welfare attitudes. The issue of enhanced government or nonprofit share of responsibility is affected as well by the uneven distribution of public and charitable policies, programs, and institutions that have evolved to carry out service, amenity, and safety net functions. The vital policy question is whether the resulting disparities in service provision between American communities are severe enough to justify reversing the decentralization strategy or limiting its scope.

The Sharing of Responsibility between Government and Nonprofits

Responsibility for addressing America's welfare, health, educational, and cultural service needs is divided between government at federal, state, and local levels and the nonprofit sector.[4] The public sector role concentrates on income transfers (at federal and state levels) to promote a more equitable distribution of income and acts to a lesser degree as a direct service provider. The nonprofit sector gives very little cash to recipients but instead provides an infrastructure for delivering services. It also develops markets in those services that can be operated without government or charitable subsidy.

America's three-sector service economy—divided between public, private, and nonprofit entities—is not a rigid and permanent structure. The division of activities has evolved over three centuries.[5] The evolution reflects the changing conditions and values of our society and the shifting comparative advantage of each of the sectors to carry out an agenda that is affected by contemporary resources, needs, and societal preferences.[6]

Even before the Great Depression of the 1930s, nonprofit leaders and philanthropists recognized that structural causes of poverty or even highly localized concentrations of poverty could not be sufficiently addressed through their modest resources and decentralized and fragmented structure.[7] Federal and state governments had to assume greater responsibility for maintaining safety nets during the Depression because charitable contributions could not meet the unprecedented social needs. With federal and state government acceptance of a more prominent distributive role, nonprofits had greater liberty to pursue activities more suited to their localized bases of support. Local autonomy permitted donations to be channeled primarily into civic and community services that enhanced the variety and quality of life.

Since World War II, government has assumed a gradually increasing share of the support for nonprofit hospitals, universities, and cultural institutions. In turn, many nonprofits now conduct activities that were traditionally in the private sector, and many private businesses are offering services in competition with nonprofit organizations. However, despite some flux in the division of responsibility between the three sectors, shifts now take place only at the margins rather than at the core of their specialized functions.

In the decades prior to the 1980s, the federal government grew more concerned with maintaining safety nets; funding social, health, educational, and cultural services; and reducing the disparities in quality of life between the nation's richer and poorer groups and regions. Government policies and programs reflected greater attention to national standards of equity and federal support to assure their implementation. While government became more reluctant in the 1980s to pursue a distributive agenda, the nonprofit sector lacked both the resources and the infrastructure to assume a larger intercommunity or national welfare role.

The Debate over Decentralization

The most serious recent challenge to the stability of the three-sector relationship occurred with the New Federalism, or decentralization, proposals in the late 1970s and 1980s. Decentralization aimed to reduce the scope of the federal government by shifting the locus of many activities to state and local government, nonprofits, and private-public partnerships. The New Federalism proposals triggered much opposition, especially from groups that equated a reduced federal role with a reduced emphasis on equity among social groups and regions. They feared that delegating authority to states and localities would lead to greater inequity in the provision and delivery of services because of the uneven distribution of both resources and service commitments. Furthermore, they believed that nonprofits could not be relied on because of their fragmented structure, uneven distribution, and inadequate resource base.

Supporters of decentralization pointed to its potential benefits, which appeared to be significant as well. Preferences and needs for specific services are not uniform throughout the nation. Decentralization can facilitate efficiency in service provision through greater attention to local preferences. In addition, services are often less costly to fund, administer, and evaluate at smaller scales. Local control can also improve funding because contributors (of taxes and voluntary donations) can more easily participate in allocation decisions and witness the benefits of the expenditures in their own communities. This argument suggests that one's neighbors are likely to be better witnesses of need and more apt to be generous than those who are more distant and remote.

An enhanced local and regional policy locus should have had especially beneficial effects for services that contribute to local amenities and civic pride, such as art centers, concert halls, and specialty hospitals. Indeed, during the 1980s a number of communities were able to launch highly successful public-private financing of new arts and cultural centers and medical and higher education facilities. But opponents argued that the national ethos, Congress, and the courts could not tolerate extreme regional and local disparities in welfare, health, educational, and cultural services. The national government could not abdicate responsibility for maintaining safety nets and quality of life to the vagaries of state and local finance, politics, and charitable instincts. The opposition arguments also reflected the suspicion that decentralization and privatization were motivated more by the expectation of cost savings than concern with improved service delivery. And early evidence provided by the Advisory Commission on Intergovernmental Relations, the Urban Institute, state and local governments, and nonprofit officials all projected dire consequences in terms of service delivery.

Others were sympathetic to the concerns of decentralization but were cautious about the hazards of rapid change. They felt Washington had grown too large and intrusive, mandating programs without attention to local concerns or differences. Taking an intermediate position, they argued that devolution merited a range of demonstration studies across the various service sectors and regional contexts to assess the best opportunities for improved and affordable service delivery.

Controlling Leviathan

Public finance and public-choice specialists have theorized about the benefits of decentralization as a strategy for reducing domestic public expenditures or at least controlling their growth.[8] Some arguments suggest that the monopoly power of central government to maximize tax revenues can be reduced through public sector decentralization. The decentralized government units, presumably at state and local levels, are forced to compete to attract and retain households and firms by offering good value (that is, direct benefit) in services per tax dollar.[9]

This "public-choice approach" presumes that state and local jurisdictions will configure taxes and service provision to satisfy preferences of residents and also to avoid repelling firms and households that might relocate to other jurisdictions with better value in services. Local support for public services and amenities valued by median voters is an investment in community improvement and may justify higher public expenditures. In contrast, state and local generosity in distributive programs and services would be expected to have a magnet effect in attracting more low-income residents and repelling higher-income and mobile households and firms.

Empirical findings do not consistently validate the decentralization strategy as a mechanism for controlling the growth of public expenditure at the national level; they do demonstrate that decentrist policies are not value-neutral. In other words, policies can be devised and altered to reflect community preferences. For example, after generous AFDC states received a considerable net in-migration of AFDC-eligible households, many reduced the generosity of their aid as well as their state and municipally financed general assistance programs. In the current recession, sixteen states have reduced their AFDC payments and general assistance grants and/or tightened eligibility. States, therefore, now differ significantly in their AFDC eligibility requirements and in their assessments of a reasonable standard of living that they are willing to underwrite for their AFDC recipients. Peterson and Rom show that AFDC benefits vary by four times as much as the differences in cost of living (two times if food stamp payments are included).

The total national expenditures for AFDC and general assistance has been reduced or limited by the participation of states and localities in setting payment levels and eligibility requirements. Presumably, according to this projection, more complete decentralization of redistributive programs should lead to a new equilibrium in which aggregate national transfers are reduced because generosity standards are cut back to the levels of the more parsimonious places. In short, the whole would be less than the sum of its parts.

Even as the income gap between poorer and more affluent communities widened in the 1980s, local government, faced with a relative decline in federal and state revenue sharing and aid, has had to take over a larger share of public service costs.[10] The federal devolution and decentralization strategies have translated the growing income gap into a widening of fiscal disparities between local jurisdictions and reduced the ability (and the incentive) of the poorer places to compensate for federal cutbacks. A decentralization strategy thus effectively reinforces cuts in federal expenditures to the poor. But it appears to be a kinder and gentler approach because the onus for cutbacks in equity-based programs is transferred to the generous and more liberal localities and the effects are likely to be felt more slowly. The Family Support Act, Supplemental Security Income (SSI), Food Stamps, and countless other programs all face highly disparate environments for state and local matching funds.

At the aggregate level, charitable contributions and voluntary efforts increased somewhat over the past decade but fell far short of compensating for the reduced public expenditures. Some nonprofits maintained their commitment to cross-subsidies, and others "creamed" more affluent clients from private providers and "dumped" their neediest recipients on public sector agencies. In some states and localities, nonprofits have been very effective lobbyists, even for support of programs of dubious effectiveness. The large and well-established nonprofits in all service sectors generally experienced considerable growth in the 1980s, but budgets for smaller and fledgling social service organizations in inner cities, for the most part, declined severely.

Some states and localities tried to make up for federal cutbacks, while others reduced their own contributions.[11] In the boom of the mid-1980s, for example, very few states or localities passed on the benefits of prosperity through transfers or service support to their lowest-income residents.

But the 1980s shift in federal redistributive politics (involving both retrenchment and accelerated decentralization) has clearly had far reaching equity consequences. Could these effects have been readily predictable from public finance theory and from the experience of the nonprofit sector?

4.

Decentralization in the Nonprofit Sector

A merican private generosity is expressed by its volunteerism and the $125 billion donated each year to nonprofit organizations. Donations help to support the educational, welfare, health, cultural, and other services performed by the 400,000 nonprofit organizations primarily engaged in service provision.[1] These organizations, widely distributed throughout the United States, employ 6 percent of the labor force and receive total revenues of $600 billion. (The other $475 billion in revenues come from fees for services government grants and contracts, interest income, and so forth.) In general, nonprofits have developed a specialized service niche that complements the services provided by government and the private sector. Nonprofit revenues from charitable contributions are supplemented by user and membership fees and government grants and contracts to compensate them for the direct services they carry out on behalf of the public interest.

Local Control of Nonprofits

The nonprofit sector is overwhelmingly community based and locally operated. In general, locally raised funds are not systematically allocated to service sectors according to prescribed formulas. However, community foundations and federated agencies like the United Way often assume the function of negotiating allocations, at least among human service providers, which must compete with one another for community donations. Communities are largely on their own to raise funds for services desired by residents without being able to count upon contributions by outsiders. Revenues are substantially raised and spent in the same communities or metropolitan areas, and there is generally little leakage between these areas except when localized natural disasters lead to national (although temporary) relief efforts.

Some important exceptions to local autonomy do occur. Many of the largest philanthropic foundations and corporations allocate their grants nationally. A number of large campaigns are nationally integrated but operate through state and local chapters, including the American Cancer Society; the Heart, Diabetes, and Muscular Dystrophy associations; the Red Cross and Planned Parenthood. Some church groups and charities also conduct national fundraising campaigns based upon prior agreements covering the division of proceeds between local groups and national or international organizations. University fundraising activities may also be integrated at a national level.

No precise measures are available on the proportion of donations that are both raised and spent locally, but estimates range from 85 to 90 percent. The national health and overseas relief campaigns alone raise only about 6 percent of the $125 billion of total annual donations. Since allocation decisions are made locally, highest priority is given to local preferences rather than to disparities in wealth, distress, or service access among communities.

Decentralized autonomy in fundraising and allocation had a more distributive effect when communities were a blend of rich and poor. However, decades of urban flight and suburbanization have yielded a high degree of income and wealth segregation. In turn, there are now distinctive agendas for nonprofit services. The focus of fundraising in affluent communities can be targeted to diverse tastes through serving specialized markets for amenities not provided by private or public sectors. In the large cities, contributions are more likely to be allocated for charitable purposes but at the expense of amenity services. But neither local resources nor the magnitude of nonprofit efforts in the poorest large cities are by themselves large enough to address structural or deeply seated social problems. Nonprofits can play only a minor role by providing the infrastructure for publicly supported human service programs.

Decentralized autonomy in the nonprofit sector can be seen as a mechanism for maximizing the level of donations. A more centralized scheme might reduce donations because donors would realize less direct benefits from their contributions. Centralization would jeopardize support for many highly valued local cultural, education, and health organizations whose claims for support may not be able to compete with preferences and priorities at metropolitan, state, or national levels.

The predominant role of nonprofits is to provide the services and amenities communities prefer rather than to act as a charitable agent. The community base allows the individual nonprofit organizations to have local autonomy and remain independent from one another. Their local autonomy has parallels to the public service functions of local government.

Distributive (that is, equity-based) activities, on the other hand, are more effectively managed at higher jurisdictional tiers. The nonprofit experience with decentralization should provide a powerful rationale for efforts to redress the equity balance at a national level. Donors to nonprofits in residential communities that are increasingly segregated by income and class want to enjoy the services provided from their contributions and not support the welfare and human service needs of those in poorer areas.

Donations to Nonprofit Organizations

The $125 billion in donations that nonprofits received in 1991 included 82.7 percent from individuals, 6.2 percent from bequests, 4.9 percent from corporations, and 6.2 percent from foundations.[2] This total represented a 31 percent real increase from 1981, but much of the gain occurred between 1981 and 1986 (see Table 1*). Donations rose from 1.84 percent of gross domestic product (GDP) in 1981 to 2.12 percent in 1986 and 2.20 percent in 1991. As a basis for comparison, this equaled about one-fifth of food expenditures. Donations for religious institutions accounted for the largest share, followed by education, health, human services, and arts and culture. While donations to religious institutions accounted for 45 percent of giving in 1981, in 1991 they equaled 54 percent, an increase largely attributable to capital campaigns for building and construction. Contributions for education, arts and culture, and civic purposes rose steeply during the decade, but donations for health services declined, and gifts for human service providers rose by only 10 percent over the decade.

While virtually all support of religious institutions comes from donations, contributions account for only 15 percent of nonprofit education revenues (mainly for higher education). Other revenues are principally derived from a combination of user fees and membership dues. The same is true for other categories, where fees, dues, government grants and contracts, and endowment income are the main revenue sources. In fact, contributions account for only 4 percent of the revenues for voluntary health agencies and hospitals, 19 percent of social service income, and 35 percent of revenues of arts and cultural institutions.

---

* Tables begin on page 41.

Overall, voluntary donations rose only modestly at a time of government cutbacks, especially in human services. The federal government was estimated to have reduced its expenditures for social services, training, education, and community development by 9 percent in the 1980s.[3] These numbers also reaffirm the notion that the label "charitable giving" includes support for a variety of services and amenities that are not truly equity based.

The Nonprofit Sector as an Example of Decentralization

Is the decentralized structure of the American nonprofit sector a model worthy of emulation and imitation by the federal government? After all, local autonomy in the nonprofit sector enables charitable agencies to effectively match local preferences for services with revenues for their provision. The nonprofit sector is even more decentralized than local government and the market-based economy; in addition, it has many other attributes that are favored by opponents of big central government.

Yet, this fragmentation of nonprofits is a reflection of their modest and specialized niche in our three-sector service economy. Responsibility for maintaining safety nets and funding health and social services still resides primarily with national (and secondarily with state and local) government. The nominal role of the nonprofit sector as an agent of distributive transfers has largely been ceded to a federated welfare state that takes more or less of the responsibility for maintaining safety nets, depending on national and state political climates and mandates. Would further federal decentralization of income transfers and service programs be able to capture the benefits of local control and fiscal oversight demonstrated by the nonprofit sector without increasing fiscal disparities and service inequities between communities? Are there any special insights to be derived from the experience of the fragmented nonprofit sector, which is so decentralized and resistant to integration at the national level?

Fragmentation in the Nonprofit Sector

The argument that the nonprofit sector has remained decentralized to serve its local donor base and to minimize redistributive transfers within, as well as between, local communities suggests that nonprofits in increasingly income-segregated communities are forced to compete for gifts and member fees by offering good value (that is, direct benefit) to contributors in services per donated dollar. Communities that are generous in their cross-subsidies and transfers would experience the magnet effect and must sooner or later yield to the standards of the more frugal localities. Generosity differences between communities in either public or nonprofit sectors must then be temporary and transitional, as places adjust to a common level. Presumably, communities pay a very high price by persisting with either public or nonprofit services that are targeted more to human services and the poor than to cultural, educational, and health care amenities.

In fact, the nonprofit sector has many other attributes worthy of emulation by the public sector if the objective is to heighten voluntary participation and oversight in local government and limit expenditures for distributive transfers. Nonprofits fit the criteria of "clubs," much like the public-choice concept of local government.[4] In the government sector, residents must move to another political jurisdiction to gain more direct and personal value from payment of local taxes. They must "vote with their feet." However, residential sorting in suburban communities by income and wealth can have the effect of equating local taxes with "voluntary" payments (analogous to contributions) for desired services. Achievement of better value is far simpler and easier for donors to nonprofit museums and for church members. They do not have to move their residence but need only shift their support to other organizations or become free-riders by continuing to enjoy the benefits of services without contributing to their support. The nonprofit sector is voluntary and noncoercive, does not issue entitlements nor guarantee safety nets, and has no formal obligations to other localities or the national society.

The U.S. nonprofit sector has never been centralized nor even highly integrated nationally. Management decisions are taken unilaterally by the hundreds of thousands of separate nonprofit organizations. Allocation decisions within the limits of the tax code are prerogatives of boards of trustees and professional management of the separate agencies. By and large, the sector has neither a hierarchical structure nor distinctive regional tiers with discretion over allocation of contributions.

The effects of the highly fragmented structure of the nonprofit sector are not difficult to determine. First, it is necessary to show that levels of donor generosity vary significantly from place-to-place. Second, one must show that donor contributions and their targeting are more amenity driven than charitable. Third, it is important to show the fragmentation effect of suburbanization, which has increasingly segregated the population by income and class and thus obviated the need or the basis for equity-based services or cross-subsidies within communities.

And finally, one must show that distributive generosity has been reduced over time in the more generous places, or diverted to amenity support. The difficulty, as with an examination of the government sector, is demonstrating that the observed changes are attributable to a decentralized structure rather than other confounding factors such as a recession or crowd-out effects of public programs.

5.

Place-to-Place Variations in Generosity

T he comparative analysis of local and regional giving patterns is important because the vast majority of giving is both solicited and expended at the community or regional level. For purposes of the comparative place-to-place analysis, individuals are aggregated over metropolitan statistical areas (MSAs). The metropolitan area, including central cities and suburbs, most accurately captures the support base for nonprofit services and their clients and is the unit generally used for fundraising campaigns.

The analysis is confined to the eighty-five largest MSAs (those with more than 500,000 residents in 1980) and their respective thirty-five states, as well as the District of Columbia. The cutoff at 500,000 was selected to exclude the smaller metropolitan areas that are not at a threshold size to have a full complement of urbanized services and amenities. These eighty-five largest metropolitan areas accounted for about 65 percent of the U.S. population in 1990.

Data Resources

A major challenge is the assembly of an adequate data set for the analyses. Data resources have improved significantly in the past decade but are still not adequate. More national fundraising organizations and umbrella groups report annual donation levels by market areas than was true ten years ago. Some limited use can also be made of the

Independent Sector's tabulations of Form 990 reporting of charitable contributions (classified by zip codes) and taxonomy system. The availability of some annual data series for selected categories of donations makes it possible to examine trends in metropolitan giving patterns that can be related to social and economic changes taking place in these communities.

Improved and up-dated data series on public sector indicators of generosity are also available from the Advisory Commission on Intergovernmental Relations (ACIR), censuses of government and services, and reports issued by associations of state and local governments. Information from the 1990 census about the metropolitan areas is helpful for constructing the control variables that assess community affluence, distress, and other socioeconomic indicators.

Variations in the Generosity of Places

The decentralized structure of the nonprofit sector suggests that the level and variety of services available to community residents are affected by the generosity of donors in that community, and not all communities are equally generous. The analysis presented here examines these variations and determines if the variations are stable or declining (as a result of magnet effects) for charitable donations as opposed to amenity contributions.

Satisfactory data for examining place-to-place differences would include donations targeted to service sectors in each community, along with the income distribution and public sector service support in the same communities. However, most donor data are not aggregated by place. To examine differences in donations, United Way (UW) contributions per employee in America's eighty-five largest MSAs are used here for the years 1972, 1986, and 1989, when slightly over $3 billion was raised nationally (see Table 2).

These data show an extreme range in contributions per employee: an eighteenfold difference from the most to the least generous places in 1972, and a thirteenfold difference in 1986 and 1989. Donation levels were highest in the smaller MSAs with half to 1 million population. Analyses indicate a significant negative relationship between 1972 contribution levels and their changes from 1972 to 1986 and from 1986 to 1989 (see Table 3). Strong and consistent differences in contribution rates persisted over the entire period but were diminished over time by a relative decline in giving in the most generous places.

United Way donations per employee have remained greater in the smaller and lower-income metropolitan areas with higher concentrations of poverty populations in the MSA center cities. However, donations increased with metropolitan income growth during the 1970s and 1980s and declined with increased metropolitan poverty and unemployment levels. The strong United Way base of higher donations in the Rustbelt (for example, Cleveland, Cincinnati, and Toledo) and in metropolitan areas with a strong corporate presence in fundraising (for example, Rochester, Minneapolis, and Hartford) is gradually eroding without compensatory growth of donations in the Sunbelt and the more suburbanized metropolitan areas (for example, Austin, Bergen County, Nassau-Suffolk, and Fort Lauderdale). These results at least partly confirm the assumption that charity rises with affluence and declines with distress.

United Way statistics are not ideal indicators of community generosity because of their focus at places of employment and the variations in how campaigns are organized.[1] Thus, separate corroboration of the variations is needed with other data series. Comparable data were available on donations to Jewish Federated Campaigns that also have a local structure for fundraising in the same MSAs for 1981, 1986, and 1990 (see Table 2). These are total contributions to local Federations, divided by the estimated Jewish population in the metropolitan area. The analysis indicates that donation levels were highly correlated (.48) with United Way contributions in the same places (see Table 3). The data also indicate similar extreme ranges from the most to the least generous places (a forty-five-fold difference) and the same significant trend toward smoothing of differences.[2] Similar findings were made for the Catholic Campaign for Human Development.

Data on giving levels for the American Kidney Foundation and the American Foundation for AIDS Research tell a similar story (see Table 2). Donations for kidney research average only one cent per capita across the eighty-five MSAs, but their range is fifty times between the least and most generous places. The range is forty times for donors to AIDS research. Furthermore, places that are generous in United Way and Federation donations (that is, smaller MSAs) are less generous donors to kidney and AIDS research that have higher participation rates in the largest and most affluent West and East Coast metropolitan areas (see Table 3).

The composite of findings for these distinct data series tends to provide additional confirmation for the hypotheses concerning:

- the significant place-to-place differences in nonprofit generosity levels;

- the positive relationship of donations to per capita income changes;

- the smoothing trend in rates of giving across the metropolitan areas; and

- the differences in giving patterns for human services (that is, UW, Federation, and so forth) in the smaller and less affluent metropolitan areas, as opposed to the disease campaigns, which find more generous donors in the larger and more affluent places.

The negative findings are revealing as well. Neither distress nor affluence, nor a politically conservative constituency, yields consistent private generosity at metropolitan levels.

Data available at the state level only (including per capita contributions to the American Diabetes, Cancer, Heart, AIDS Research, and Planned Parenthood associations, and for Public TV and Radio) show similar close associations in donation levels according to income levels and wide variations between the most and least generous states (see Table 4). Furthermore, except for Heart Association donations, giving levels are significantly higher in the more liberal than in the more traditional and conservative states.

These findings provide at least partial evidence for arguing that decentralization of voluntary contributions for human services makes recipients of such services vulnerable to wide differences in local generosity. The analysis cannot, however, confirm the notion that the most generous communities are forced to cut back generosity levels because of a magnet effect. Clearly, low-income people are very unlikely to make migration decisions solely on the basis of United Way, Jewish Federation, or Catholic Charities support for human services or funding from the various disease campaigns. Their consistency over the range of metropolitan areas suggests, however, that local autonomy can be highly prejudicial to low-income people in the less generous places.

Charitable versus Amenity-Supporting Generosity

Local autonomy in fundraising and allocations has other implications as well. Theory would lead us to expect that the proportion of household contributions targeted to charity (that is, distributive purposes) is quite small relative to that used for amenities or church membership. The assumption here is that sustained charitable transfers are prompted more by altruistic motives than by expectations of direct or indirect benefit. In contrast, membership fees and support for amenity activities (that is, "connoisseur goods," a term coined by Albert Hirschman), even though allowable as tax deductible contributions, represent the purchase of valued services. The fact that these services are purchased from nonprofit organizations rather than in the market economy has some relevance because the fees often include cross-subsidies for lower-income users. But charitable donations are more likely than contributions for amenities to target beneficiaries with incomes lower than those of the donors.

A satisfactory data set would allow us to distinguish altruistic or charitable gifts from membership fees and support for amenities. The data series used to examine the composition of contributions were derived from the IRS 990 forms filed by nonprofit organizations in the late 1980s and classified according to the National Taxonomy of Exempt Entities (NTEE) code of agency specialization by the National Center for Charitable Statistics. The classification does not provide precise distinctions between charitable as opposed to other functional service categories.[3] Instead, a proxy measure is used based upon the share of total nonprofit expenditures, assets, and support of organizations in the "human service" category in each of the eighty-five metropolitan areas. Human services are assumed to be somewhat more charitable and redistributive than any of the other service categories.[4] However, few nonprofit human service organizations target their activities exclusively to low-income clients.[5] In fact, nonprofit human service agencies that target a larger share of their services to the poor are more likely to have government subsidies for these services than revenues from private donations.[6] Evidence shows that agency focus on the poor declines as the share of revenue from private charity increases.

The analyses indicate considerable variation between metropolitan areas in the human service share of total nonprofit support and expenditures (see Table 2). The shares are smallest in the largest metropolitan areas and where poverty is most pronounced. Furthermore, the shares are smaller where total per capita gifts and grants to nonprofit agencies are largest (see Table 3). The findings indicate that places not only vary significantly in the charitable component of their generosity but higher levels of generosity are reflected by greater relative support for amenities than for charitable purposes. The analysis also shows that nonprofits have a very modest share of human service support in both the largest and the poorest cities relative to their role in supporting amenities and relative to local, state, and federal public sector aid.

Generosity in Center Cities and Suburbs

Nonprofits can also be classified by center city and suburban locations. Those located in center cities average about three times more gifts and grants received, expenditures, and assets as those in suburban areas (and about five times as much on a per capita basis). Per capita support for AIDS and kidney research are, respectively, two times and 30 percent higher in center city than in suburban portions of MSAs. Higher poverty rates in center cities also suggest that considerable assistance is needed from suburban residents to sustain the nonprofit institutions that are concentrated in the center city. City nonprofits will be even harder pressed financially if suburbanization leads to greater loosening of ties to these institutions.

The analyses also reveal that 25 percent of support for the center-city nonprofits is targeted to human service organizations, relative to 18 percent in the suburbs. Suburbanites can spend more of their donations for civic purposes and to support arts, educational, and health facilities. The data also indicate only a modest (but not significant) relationship between the shares of nonprofit support for human services in center cities relative to their own suburbs. Growing stratification and homogenization have helped to produce different nonprofit agendas in center cities and suburban fringes.

State and Local Government Generosity

State and local government generosity is indexed by a wide variety of surrogates including expenditures for the arts per capita, the number of librarians per 10,000 employees, revenue dependency on progressive income taxes, ACIR's measure of tax effort, Medicaid expenditures and proportion of state budget devoted to public welfare relative to poverty population, AFDC payments per family, average teachers' salaries, school expenditures per child in school, and an index of educational quality (see Table 5). All these measures are highly intercorrelated and strongly related to state per capita income. The analysis of residuals from the regression equation linking these generosity measures with per capita income showed a number of states that were somewhat more generous than would be expected on the basis of their income—including Rhode Island, Indiana, and Wisconsin—and a number that were somewhat less generous than expected—including Virginia, Maryland, the District of Columbia, Nebraska, and New Jersey. However, the strong link of the measures to per capita income demonstrates how economic inequalities and fiscal disparities severely limit generous tendencies and impose quite different standards in service provision.

The Relationship between Metropolitan and State Generosity

Does generosity by the public sector crowd out private philanthropy and charitable donations? While the crowd-out issues cannot be addressed fully with the available data, the analysis does show that states that spend more on amenity services are also more generous in their financing of human services (see Table 6). The analysis also shows that greater state government spending on human services is in tandem with greater metropolitan support for nonprofit amenity services. Furthermore, a close relationship exists between metropolitan generosity in support of human services and state funding of amenity services. A reasonable interpretation of these findings suggests that the financially better off states do in fact assume a greater role in underwriting both amenity and human services at local levels. This government aid allows nonprofits to focus more on "luxuries," that is, local amenities. In states less generous in their support of human services, metropolitan nonprofits compensate through a greater focus on these more basic needs.

6.

Generosity, Affluence, and Distress

Nonprofit and government support for welfare and amenity services are very unevenly distributed across America's metropolitan areas. To what extent are these disparities explained by differences in wealth and distress, and how severe are the place-to-place differences in community resources and need? Are the regional inequalities in public and nonprofit resources, as well as generosity, severe enough either to undermine the pursuit of decentralization, or to justify selective recentralization?

The empirical analysis in this section examines whether the disparities between America's communities can be addressed through a decentrist policy of state and local public and private generosity. In other words, do American communities differ so widely in available resources, levels of distress, and social welfare values and attitudes that a decentrist strategy would be hazardous to service users in many communities?

Decentralization trades national commitment for a greater reliance on regional and local resources and service preferences. The rationale for numerous federal domestic programs in the New Deal and Fair Deal eras had been based upon the severity of inequality in the United States.[1] The concentration of the neediest people in inner cities, the rural South, Appalachia, and in parts of the Southwest were assumed to be too large a burden for purely local or regional efforts. Concentrated pockets of poverty justified national commitment and federal assistance through grants-in-aid and formula-based programs in welfare and human services, legal, housing, and health services targeted to the need-iest people and regions. Other federal assistance programs were not income based but designed to foster a variety of meritorious services in American communities to support museums, public radio and TV, science education, and similar educational and cultural activities. With greater reliance on state and local resources, communities became the determinants of appropriate service levels, making sure that service and transfer budgets would not exceed local preferences and standards of quality of life.

The model of generosity used in the analysis assumes that giving levels across the eighty-five MSAs are affected primarily by resource differences but also reflect the effects of need or distress. Just as impor-tantly, they reflect value differences expressed as social welfare prefer-ences. Generosity is a product of a surplus beyond direct consumption needs and the cost of giving. More affluent places are assumed to be more generous than needier places, but the degree of generosity also depends on the presence of relative need. Contributions are solicited to provide support for services or activities that donors deem worthy of support. The last component of the generosity model consists of social values and attitudes, both of which affect contributions to support vari-ety, diversity, and equity in community life.

The analysis of place-to-place differences in generosity also allows us to address some very general questions about giving behavior that cannot be examined with national data sets. For example, can disparities in generosity be attributed to differences in community size, wealth, income distribution, homogeneity, or some particular course of histor-ical development? Do they reflect disparate political cultures or solely the socioeconomic and demographic composition of their populations?

Estimation of the model will help us to assess the degree to which decentralization acts to increase or reduce disparities in service provision because of community differences. A finding that disparities are signif-icant in some service sectors (for example, cultural and educational ser-vices) rather than social services would have different policy implications from an outcome showing consistency across all sectors. Findings that point to generosity levels as solely attributable to wealth differences would require a policy remedy different from a finding based upon the influence of community distress.

How severe were America's regional inequalities in 1980 and how did they change over the decade? We examine these issues by looking first at some illustrative measures of the distribution of both resources and distress, then at the effects of these differences on generosity levels. The measures refer to the entire MSAs including both center cities and suburbs, and thus do not reveal the internal economic and social inequalities between them, which are generally more severe than differences between MSAs.

One of the better proxy measures of resources available for all eighty-five MSAs is the Woods and Poole Wealth Index, which includes income from employment, rents, and dividends and excludes income from transfer payments (see Table 7). The index provides a reasonable estimate of income that can be taxed at state and local levels for provision of services and income transfers. Wealth values vary considerably across the MSAs from highs in Bergen and Monmouth counties in New Jersey, San Francisco, San Jose, and Washington, D.C., to lows in Fresno, Gary, Riverside, New Orleans, Salt Lake City, and San Antonio. These latter places all lack extensive areas of affluent suburban fringe development.

The wealth differences are closely related to relative job and income growth over the 1980s (see Table 7). Metropolitan areas such as Austin, Dallas, Boston, Denver, Hartford, Nassau County (New York), San Antonio, Tampa, Orlando, and West Palm Beach were all growing rapidly in both income and employment. In contrast, slow income and job growth or decline was occurring in the industrial cities of Detroit, Akron, Birmingham, Dayton, Gary, and Youngstown.

At the state level, the ACIR index of "tax capacity" illustrates resource differences available for supplementing income transfers and contributing to state and local government services (see Table 8). The index values are closely correlated with the variations in per capita income. The values are highest in Connecticut, Massachusetts, New Jersey, and Washington, D.C. Of the states included (thirty-six of them), lowest index values occur in Alabama, Utah, and Kentucky. State rankings are also provided from a recent study from the General Accounting Office that shows the extent of local fiscal disparities, assuming no state and federal general fiscal assistance.[2] Kentucky's local fiscal disparities without such aid, for example, would be three times those of Oregon. Disparities between states tended to widen during the 1980s as per capita income rose most rapidly in the already most affluent states. Numbers on Medicaid increased by 5 percent, but there were substantial changes in their distribution during the decade, reflecting both changes in poverty levels and eligibility requirements.

The measures of distress also show significant variations across metropolitan areas. Population in the eighty-five MSAs grew by 15 million during the 1980s, but the growth was highly uneven (see Table 9). Relative growth was fastest in the Sunbelt areas, while Rustbelt MSAs such as Youngstown, Pittsburgh, and Gary experienced significant population decline. Poverty rates in 1989 were generally consistent across the MSAs with the proportion of female-headed households and other distress indicators, including the percentage of low birth weights, infant death rates, children born to teenagers, and income derived from transfer payments. The average poverty rate remained constant at 11 percent between 1979 and 1989, but differences between the MSAs generally intensified. While poverty rates grew in MSAs that experienced population growth as well as decline, virtually all the poverty increases in the growing MSAs were absorbed within their central cities.

The data tables demonstrate that America's metropolitan areas and states shared very unequally in the 1980s national growth surge. States with rapidly growing economies and tax revenues were able to assist their local governments more than those growing more slowly or in decline. Greater economic inequality between states and local governments translates into greater fiscal disparities and greater variations in ability to support basic governmental and welfare services. Shrinking economies also led to reduced public expenditures for civic and amenity services and less local support for nonprofits in the arts, education, welfare, and human service sectors.

Testing the Model of Metropolitan Generosity

The conventional wisdom is that variations in generosity levels between American communities can be readily explained by their differences in wealth and distress. These assumptions are tested in a cross-sectional (ordinary least squares) regression analysis for 1990.

1. The initial model posits that generosity (indexed by average per employee United Way contributions) in the eighty-five metropolitan areas is a function of:

    ♦ population of the metropolitan area;

    ♦ wealth (the Woods and Poole index of wages, rents, and dividends);

    ♦ a measure of corporate and civic presence (indexed by the number of Fortune 500 firms headquartered in the area);

    ♦ a surrogate for distress level (indexed by the metropolitan unemployment level); and

    ♦ social welfare ideology (as measured by the American Conservative Union index of voting records of members of Congress representing the metropolitan area).

2.   The second model has as its dependent variable:

> ◆ per capita expenditures by nonprofits across the 85
> metropolitan areas (as a proxy for nonprofit activity).

The independent variables are the same as those in the first
model, but with the addition of:

> ◆ nonprofit human services expenditures as a percent-
> age of total expenditures of nonprofit organizations
> (as a proxy for distributive generosity).

3.   The third model has as its dependent variable:

> ◆ nonprofit human services expenditures as a percent-
> age of total expenditures of nonprofit organizations
> (as a proxy for distributive generosity).

The independent variables are the same as those in the first
model, but with the addition of:

> ◆ per capita expenditures by nonprofits across the eighty-
> five metropolitan areas (as a proxy for nonprofit activity).

Do differences in wealth and distress account for the variations in
United Way generosity? The relationship to metropolitan wealth and distress is strong, but in a negative direction. Giving is higher in the less
affluent and smaller metropolitan areas, where unemployment is lower
and where Fortune 500 firms are more numerous (see Table 10). The
social ideology assumption is only weakly supported by the findings.
Contributions are only marginally higher in the more liberal districts.
These findings are not conclusive, of course, because the UW context for
donations (with an emphasis on blue-collar donors) varies so much by
community. However, the results add to our doubts about the validity of
the wealth and distress explanation for the variations in giving levels.
     The variations in expenditures by all nonprofits are only weakly
related to the measures of metropolitan wealth and distress (see Table
10). Nonprofit activity is modestly higher where Fortune 500 firms are
more prominent, where incomes are greater, and where unemployment
is lower. The results also indicate more nonprofit activity per capita in
the smaller metropolitan areas (though the coefficient is not significant). More noteworthy is the close association of nonprofit activity
levels to a more liberal ideology, the lack of relationship to UW giving
levels, and the very strong negative linkage to the share of nonprofit

expenditures in the human service sector. Despite the strong advocacy by conservatives for volunteerism and a strengthened nonprofit sector, nonprofits have a larger per capita role in liberal districts. As indicated earlier, greater prominence of nonprofit activity is associated with a smaller share targeted to human services, with greater emphasis given to nonprofit amenity sectors, such as education, culture, and health.

The share of human services among nonprofit activities is more closely related to the distribution of wealth and distress than the other indicators of private generosity (see Table 10). Human services receive a larger share in the smaller metropolitan areas, where affluence is greater, where Fortune 500 firms are more concentrated, where unemployment is higher, and where other nonprofit activities are more modest. The positive relationship to conservative political preferences is very significant. Liberals tend to support the more amenity oriented nonprofit activity, while conservatives would appear to prefer greater nonprofit focus on human services.

7.

Summary and Discussion

The post–World War II period had witnessed an evolving specialization of functions and distinctive niches for private, public,
and nonprofit service sectors and the emergence of distinctive
partnerships between these sectors. The nonprofit sector had reached
some stability in its relationship with private and public sectors prior to
the New Federalism era. But a current analysis of the rationale for the
nonprofit sector would reach quite different conclusions than studies in
the late 1970s. The growing stimulus for privatization, devolution of
federal programs to states and localities, greater reliance on the nonprofit sector as a service provider, and the Tax Reform Act of 1986 have
combined to alter fundamentally the specialized roles of the public and
nonprofit sectors and their interdependencies.

The thesis examined in this study has argued that decentralization of government support for income transfers and human services
implies a reduced emphasis on equity. The example provided by the
nonprofit sector allows us to examine the implications of an almost
completely decentralized system. Nonprofits have become locked into
a process of largely providing services and amenities to their own local
donors and are not organized to provide more generous support for
redistributive services. However, the most serious implications of decentralization for nonprofits are the impediments to retargeting support
between service sectors and from places of affluence to places of long-
term distress.

A decade of devolution and decentralization of federal programs has
already yielded considerable disparity between places because states and
municipalities vary in their fiscal resources and willingness to compensate
for federal cutbacks. Much of this effect could have been readily antici-
pated from public finance studies of fiscal federalism and the organization
of the nonprofit sector. The decentralization strategy may potentially

help to restrict central government growth, but it also reduces the prospects for consistently equitable remedies across America's communities by either public or nonprofit sectors.

Decentralization and Equity

Greater regional and local financing and control over basic services seem to be quite dysfunctional for a range of services. Federal devolution of responsibility (especially for welfare and social services) ties local and state support and matching funds to the vagaries of fiscal constraints, balanced budgets, and local and regional economic swings. Advocates on behalf of low-income and handicapped people have not been as effective being lobbyists in state legislatures and city councils as they had been in Washington in New and Fair Deal periods. Near neighbors seem often to be less generous than those more removed, especially in periods of distress. States and localities differ markedly in fiscal resources and reflect distinctive cultures of generosity that vary considerably from national values and standards. In some localities, federal cuts in assistance have been more than offset by enhancements in state and local programs, while in others the decline of federal support has been matched by even greater cuts in local aid and charitable support. Furthermore, acts of public and private generosity appear to stem more from the presence of prosperity than distress and to operate in tandem rather than as substitutes.

The available evidence shows that decentralization of programs in the past decade has reduced considerably total national subsidy levels for services as well as their distributive targeting. Some evidence points to this factor as the latent motivation for the devolution efforts. The evidence shows that service support and transfer payments now differ more by region and locale than at any time since World War II.

Disparities in quality of life and access to a diversity of cultural and educational services are growing between states and metropolitan areas. Service disparities are greatest in social and welfare services and least in health, educational, and cultural services. These indications of differences suggest that the devolution and decentrist experiment has been most painful for the lowest-income population and that state and local remedies for these problems are unlikely to be effective for many localities. Fiscal differences and variations in political cultures and institutions at state and local levels in government and voluntary sectors contribute to the inequity in service and transfer programs.

These outcomes follow a certain rationale that should have been predictable. The decentralization of discretion and funding has not adversely affected services that contribute to civic pride and local amenities, especially in more affluent regions. On the other hand, the declining metropolitan areas and states now have increased service needs but declining public and voluntary support for their provision.

The Virtues of Maintaining the Traditional Nonprofit Sector

Nonprofit organizations and their donors and volunteers accomplish a great deal in their own communities, and some even respond valiantly to crises elsewhere in the nation or overseas. Virtually all of our human services agencies and arts and cultural institutions are nonprofits, as are many of our leading universities and hospitals and all of our churches and synagogues. In general, nonprofits do an excellent job in doing exactly what they do best, which is to help support amenities and variety in American community life and supplement the services that neither the private nor public sector is able or willing to provide.

In the 1980s, Presidents Reagan and Bush repeatedly called for greater volunteerism, community giving, and a greater service role for nonprofits. Should nonprofits take over a larger share of services now performed by government and help to limit federal domestic expenditures? Market driven, nonprofit, and government sectors at national, state, and local levels each have their own comparative advantages and specialized niches in providing amenities and services. Nonprofits are not able to expand their roles and assume greater commitment for providing services targeted at our neediest population, at least not without corresponding increases in public subsidies. Furthermore, the structure of the nonprofit sector cannot serve as a model for government provision of services. In fact, greater stress on the nonprofit sector to do what it cannot do well threatens to undermine its ability to carry on its traditional functions.

Nonprofits cannot quickly induce greater donations from the American population. Contributions have not been rising much above the inflation rate for the past fifty years. The Tax Reform Act of 1986 had little effect in eliciting a higher contribution rate among our richest households (which benefited most from the new lower tax schedules). Much of the support base for nonprofit agencies comes from government grants and contracts, and this portion of their revenues is too large to be replaced by donations or client fees.

The most serious drawback of greater reliance on the nonprofit sector, however, is that it is primarily locally based and fragmented. Generosity is much greater in some communities than in others and is generally higher where affluence is greater, rather than in areas where distress is greater. Continuing suburbanization makes our communities even more homogeneous and lessens the commitment to residents of the pockets of urban and rural poverty. No capstone organization at the national, regional, or local level takes responsibility for targeting contributions where they are most seriously needed, except when national disasters occur. No responsible parties see to it that a significant share of donations are used in a "charitable" fashion, that is, for services primarily targeted to the poor or handicapped. No regulations or guidelines prevent the subsidization of amenities that primarily serve the already comfortable. In truth, very little of our tax deductible contributions is targeted to the "truly needy," especially those outside our own communities. Voluntary organizations have neither the resources to make a dent in our poverty problem nor the infrastructure to act on a national basis. These are functions that the national government is best equipped to provide, assisted by state and local governments when local preferences require specialized programs.

Nonprofits are good at innovation and demonstration. The hazard in expecting that nonprofits can take over more responsibility from government is that they will lose their traditional capacity to innovate with new program ideas and to demonstrate their advantages and pitfalls in modest undertakings before adoption at a national scale. Nonprofits are also effective in enhancing the variety and balance of our community life and in preserving the heritage and traditions of past accomplishments. They lack sufficient resources at the right sites to assume responsibility for feeding and housing the homeless, caring for those with AIDS, and teaching literacy and job skills. Salary scales have fallen in nonprofits; failure rates are higher than bankruptcy levels among comparably sized private firms. To survive, some are "creaming and dumping"—competing for clients with private sector organizations and dumping their neediest clients on the local public sector. Many have taken on fundraising activities and are flooding the mails with promotional literature. Traditional nonprofits are becoming an endangered species, and our national treasure of nonprofit institutions is being undermined.

Much of what has been said about nonprofits applies with equal relevance to the devolution of federal programs to state and local governments. In fact, the fragmented structure of local jurisdictions shares much with the atomized nonprofit sector. The shift in national leadership gives us a renewed opportunity to consider the virtues of some selective recentralization of service responsibility, especially for those programs targeted to maintaining safety nets. Much of the national support for subsidizing amenities can perhaps remain decentralized because local civic pride can often be relied upon to sustain institutions that provide locally valued services. But the pockets of local distress should not rely purely upon local resources and generosity of spirit.

TABLE 1
CHARITABLE DONATIONS BY SERVICE SECTOR, 1981–91
(IN BILLIONS OF 1991 DOLLARS)

| | 1981 | 1986 | 1991 | Percentage Change | | |
				1981–86	1986–91	1981–91
Religion	42.97	52.96	67.59	23	28	57
Education	9.90	11.93	13.28	21	11	34
Health	9.93	10.72	9.68	8	-10	-3
Human services	9.64	11.60	10.61	20	-9	10
Arts, culture	6.28	7.41	8.81	18	19	40
Civic	3.07	3.11	4.93	1	59	61
Environment	NA	NA	2.54	NA	NA	NA
International	NA	NA	2.59	NA	NA	NA
Undesignated	13.72	17.45	4.74	27	-73	-65
Total	95.50	115.19	124.77	21	8	31

Source: '92 Giving USA. AAFRC Trust for Philanthropy, 1992.
Note: The "undesignated" catagory is not comparable because of definitional changes.
NA = not available.

TABLE 2

PRIVATE GENEROSITY MEASURES FOR METROPOLITAN AREAS

Metropolitan Area	UW 89	UW 72	UW 72–89	Fed 90	Fed 81	Fed 81–90	NP Supp	Human	Kidney	AIDS	Con-serv
Akron	41	30	1.35	272	195	1.39	0.22	0.25	0.006	0.25	11
Albany	22	16	1.41	NA	111	NA	0.85	0.04	0.017	0.51	46
Allentown	32	NA	NA	306	228	1.34	0.26	0.14	0.011	0.25	55
Anaheim–Santa Ana	16	8	1.83	18	18	1.00	0.14	0.23	0.013	0.64	92
Atlanta	38	14	2.69	161	107	1.50	0.47	0.10	0.006	0.53	52
Austin	19	8	2.28	81	62	1.31	0.20	0.25	0.011	0.58	47
Baltimore	33	11	2.93	228	131	1.74	0.29	0.18	0.015	0.35	34
Bergen–Passaic	13	4	2.99	139	88	1.58	0.15	0.24	0.016	0.71	29
Birmingham	41	16	2.62	466	304	1.53	0.18	0.15	0.004	0.19	57
Boston	38	11	3.32	120	80	1.50	1.15	0.08	0.008	0.62	9
Buffalo	38	18	2.09	182	129	1.41	0.29	0.23	0.012	0.36	38
Charlotte	44	13	3.40	311	148	2.10	0.30	0.12	0.006	0.54	55
Chicago	33	12	2.65	218	140	1.55	0.43	0.14	0.013	0.55	36
Cincinnati	60	21	2.90	241	163	1.48	0.32	0.19	0.008	0.34	58
Cleveland	69	24	2.83	387	272	1.42	0.44	0.16	0.010	0.36	10
Columbus	59	14	4.09	417	214	1.95	0.37	0.22	0.009	0.37	85
Dallas	38	13	2.84	177	241	0.73	0.37	0.12	0.007	0.48	60
Dayton	49	21	2.35	330	214	1.54	0.20	0.14	0.007	0.45	70
Denver	37	13	2.87	112	131	0.85	0.31	0.13	0.007	0.50	55
Detroit	36	22	1.67	284	268	1.06	0.27	0.17	0.008	0.28	21
Fort Lauderdale	13	6	2.03	69	60	1.14	0.10	NA	0.002	0.34	39
Fort Worth	39	15	2.69	169	209	0.81	0.16	0.30	0.007	0.26	67
Fresno	6	6	0.93	NA	NA	NA	0.23	0.37	0.007	0.18	33
Gary	27	15	1.73	322	304	1.06	0.14	0.37	0.006	0.14	15
Grand Rapids	41	13	3.19	304	256	1.19	0.42	0.21	0.014	0.42	74
Greensboro–Winston-Salem	56	15	3.72	372	322	1.16	0.16	0.19	0.007	0.18	48
Greenville–Spartanburg	35	11	3.24	NA	NA	NA	0.26	NA	0.008	NA	44
Harrisburg	45	14	3.20	302	225	1.34	0.26	0.44	0.015	0.48	94
Hartford	71	NA	NA	263	180	1.46	0.44	0.20	0.008	0.57	18
Honolulu	45	17	2.66	48	NA	NA	0.31	0.22	0.023	0.70	54

TABLE 2 (Continued)

Metropolitan Area	UW 89	UW 72	UW 72–89	Fed 90	Fed 81	Fed 81–90	NP Supp	Human	Kidney	AIDS	Con-serv
Houston	38	12	3.27	170	170	1.00	0.24	NA	0.006	0.24	51
Indianapolis	44	14	3.06	417	263	1.59	0.29	0.21	0.008	0.31	57
Jacksonville	31	13	2.37	151	156	0.97	0.24	0.32	0.006	0.33	60
Jersey City	10	NA	NA	NA	66	NA	0.57	0.27	0.050	2.91	13
Kansas City	39	13	2.99	213	156	1.37	0.28	0.25	0.008	NA	45
Kansas City MO	43	16	2.65	213	156	1.37	NA	NA	0.008	NA	40
Knoxville	36	13	2.75	243	140	1.74	0.22	0.11	0.007	0.19	72
Los Angeles	22	9	2.37	101	75	1.35	0.36	NA	0.001	2.22	35
Louisville	38	NA	NA	250	224	1.12	0.31	0.13	0.010	0.36	38
Memphis	39	16	2.45	263	156	1.69	0.33	0.13	0.005	0.29	35
Miami	24	13	1.93	80	76	1.05	0.33	0.16	0.014	0.82	21
Middlesex–Somerset	41	6	6.95	87	46	1.88	0.14	0.28	0.011	0.47	48
Milwaukee	37	19	1.96	322	300	1.07	0.31	0.38	0.013	0.32	38
Minneapolis	51	25	2.04	436	324	1.35	0.35	0.22	0.009	NA	26
Monmouth–Ocean	7	2	2.74	54	31	1.75	0.11	0.18	0.014	0.51	41
Nashville	41	16	2.59	510	338	1.51	0.33	0.15	0.005	0.20	40
Nassau–Suffolk	7	4	1.75	NA	101	NA	0.20	0.28	0.018	NA	24
New Haven	28	18	1.54	131	94	1.39	0.69	0.15	0.021	1.19	25
New Orleans	32	13	2.51	200	182	1.10	0.16	0.30	0.005	0.28	57
New York City	26	NA	NA	73	56	1.31	0.97	0.12	0.020	NA	10
Newark	38	NA	NA	258	105	2.45	0.12	0.19	0.002	0.10	34
Norfolk	39	13	2.92	145	132	1.10	0.25	0.04	0.008	0.42	56
Oakland	28	NA	NA	93	70	1.33	0.21	0.29	0.009	0.95	4
Oklahoma City	29	NA	NA	199	382	0.52	0.26	0.13	0.004	0.26	59
Omaha	44	16	2.80	382	289	1.32	0.28	0.17	0.007	0.35	61
Orlando	18	NA	NA	108	142	0.76	0.22	0.25	0.012	0.51	66
Oxnard–Ventura	16	NA	NA	NA	NA	NA	0.19	0.38	0.009	0.82	92
Philadelphia	35	16	2.11	119	86	1.38	0.38	0.15	0.010	0.51	28
Phoenix	23	8	2.80	84	61	1.38	0.19	NA	0.006	0.34	65
Pittsburgh	42	NA	NA	211	175	1.21	0.40	0.13	0.013	0.27	23
Portland	28	14	1.96	233	177	1.32	0.26	0.18	0.008	0.41	30
Providence	27	20	1.38	269	195	1.38	0.71	0.20	0.011	0.57	25

TABLE 2 (Continued)

Metropolitan Area	UW 89	UW 72	UW 72–89	Fed 90	Fed 81	Fed 81–90	NP Supp	Human	Kidney	AIDS	Con-serv
Raleigh	32	10	3.19	55	28	1.97	0.87	0.09	0.010	0.52	32
Richmond	40	9	4.49	338	227	1.49	0.38	0.42	0.015	0.39	75
Riverside	17	13	1.36	NA	NA	NA	0.07	0.25	0.003	0.16	57
Rochester	74	36	2.05	155	134	1.16	0.39	0.15	0.012	0.34	38
Sacramento	19	8	2.25	93	65	1.43	0.15	0.31	0.007	0.36	32
Salt Lake City	14	8	1.67	123	164	0.75	0.10	0.29	0.003	0.21	62
San Antonio	41	11	3.63	152	198	0.77	0.20	0.22	0.006	0.41	41
San Diego	25	12	2.10	143	106	1.35	0.21	0.27	0.006	0.68	61
San Francisco	28	12	2.31	137	155	0.88	1.16	0.11	0.016	3.15	18
San Jose	30	9	3.49	52	48	1.08	0.21	0.45	0.005	0.48	23
Scranton	27	13	2.07	392	301	1.30	0.15	0.16	0.005	0.14	54
Seattle	44	NA	NA	235	127	1.85	0.27	0.24	0.004	0.44	25
Springfield	42	NA	NA	173	152	1.14	0.46	0.36	0.008	0.61	13
St. Louis	47	23	2.09	191	126	1.52	0.30	0.13	0.010	0.32	36
Syracuse	37	18	2.07	159	128	1.24	0.34	0.23	0.010	0.32	42
Tampa	19	11	1.78	100	82	1.22	0.18	0.08	0.004	0.18	67
Toledo	41	27	1.56	268	226	1.19	0.27	0.17	0.010	0.22	41
Tucson	45	17	2.72	115	86	1.34	0.22	0.24	0.011	0.41	33
Tulsa	55	NA	NA	808	1,294	0.62	0.43	0.10	0.006	0.24	48
West Palm Beach	23	NA	NA	179	66	2.72	0.20	NA	0.024	0.91	58
Washington	34	11	3.14	123	82	1.50	1.01	NA	0.025	1.21	52
Wilmington	62	28	2.24	136	100	1.36	0.22	0.38	0.011	0.32	23
Youngstown	30	16	1.92	369	279	1.32	0.12	0.30	0.003	0.13	21

UW 89 and UW 72 = United Way contributions per employee in 1989 and 1972; UW 72–89 = their relative changes between 1972 and 1989. *Source:* United Way of America.

Fed 90, Fed 81, and Fed 81–90 = Contributions per Jewish resident to Federation in 1990 and 1981, and the relative changes between 1981 and 1990. *Source:* Council of Jewish Federations.

NP Supp = Gifts and grants to metropolitan nonprofits per capita, 1989. *Source:* Independent Sector.

Human = Share of gifts and grants to nonprofits accounted for by human service agencies, 1989. *Source:* Independent Sector.

Kidney = Donations per capita to the American Kidney Foundation, 1990.

AIDS = Donors per capita to the American Foundation for AIDS Research, 1990.

Conserv = American Conservative Union rating of district House members, 1990.

TABLE 3

CORRELATION OF GENEROSITY MEASURES IN THE 85 LARGEST MSAs

Variables	UW 89	UW 86	UW 72	UW 72–89	Fed 90	Fed 81	Fed 81–90	NP Supp	Human	Kidney	AIDS	Wealth
UW 89	*	0.95	0.73	0.21	0.48	0.43	0.36	0.08	-0.16	-0.17	-0.26	-0.14
UW 86		*	0.73	0.14	0.44	0.39	0.30	0.05	-0.12	-0.19	-0.28	-0.14
UW 72			*	-0.30	0.38	0.41	0.41	0.09	-0.14	0.00	-0.17	-0.30
UW 72–89				*	-0.05	-0.19	-0.19	-0.02	0.10	0.11	0.03	0.47
Fed 90					*	0.84	0.04	-0.08	-0.09	-0.24	-0.32	-0.34
Fed 81						*	-0.34	-0.13	-0.03	-0.29	-0.33	-0.46
Fed 81–90							*	-0.05	-0.10	-0.21	-0.23	-0.33
NP Supp								*	-0.41	0.41	0.52	0.26
Human									*	0.04	-0.03	0.00
Kidney										*	0.60	0.30
AIDS											*	0.41
Wealth												*

Coefficients >0.19 are significant at 90% level
>0.23 are significant at 95%
>0.29 are significant at 99%

UW 89, UW 86, and UW 72 = United Way contributions per employee in 1989, 1986, and 1972; UW 72–89 = their relative changes between 1972 and 1989. *Source:* United Way of America.

Fed 90, Fed 81, and Fed 81–90 = Contributions per Jewish resident to Federation in 1990 and 1981, and the relative changes between 1981 and 1990. *Source:* Council of Jewish Federations.

NP Supp = Gifts and grants to metropolitan nonprofits per capita, 1989. *Source:* Independent Sector.

Human = Share of gifts and grants to nonprofits accounted for by human service agencies, 1989. *Source:* Independent Sector.

Kidney = Donations per capita to the American Kidney Foundation, 1990.

AIDS = Donors per capita to the American Foundation for AIDS Research, 1990.

Wealth = Woodes and Poole wealth index, 1990.

TABLE 4
STATE MEASURES OF GENEROSITY (35 STATES AND THE DISTRICT OF COLUMBIA)

State	Diabetes	Heart	Cancer	Public TV	Public Radio	Planned Parenthood	AIDS	Moral	Indiv	Trad
Alabama	0.38	6.66	65.50	0.25	0.03	0.01	42.19	0	1	1
Arizona	1.15	4.78	137.20	1.24	0.05	0.06	155.22	1	0	1
California	0.81	3.76	95.10	1.61	0.01	0.15	NA	1	0	0
Colorado	0.67	2.63	98.40	1.25	0.13	0.09	101.61	1	0	0
Connecticut	0.90	5.79	160.10	0.88	0.11	0.09	428.68	1	1	0
Delaware	0.77	7.69	200.10	NA	NA	0.13	122.03	0	1	1
District of Columbia*	1.34	13.47	120.30	13.00	6.38	0.54	501.28	NA	NA	NA
Florida	0.32	4.40	120.20	0.72	0.01	0.05	381.98	0	1	1
Georgia	0.57	5.16	135.80	0.08	0.01	0.03	108.80	0	1	1
Hawaii	0.50	11.50	196.20	0.63	0.30	0.15	136.88	0	1	1
Illinois	0.59	3.45	89.00	1.25	0.01	0.06	439.00	1	1	0
Indiana	0.77	4.45	69.90	0.55	0.02	0.03	96.38	0	1	0
Kansas	0.83	6.11	112.30	0.64	0.10	0.05	253.01	1	1	0
Kentucky	0.31	4.07	51.70	0.73	0.05	0.02	72.07	0	1	1
Louisiana	0.36	2.66	24.50	0.53	0.04	0.01	89.69	0	1	1
Maryland	1.46	5.32	120.30	0.64	0.04	0.33	222.28	0	1	1
Massachusetts	0.31	4.21	106.40	2.35	0.09	0.30	185.31	1	1	0
Michigan	0.70	2.30	81.80	1.14	0.03	0.05	486.98	1	0	0
Minnesotta	1.48	5.35	143.20	1.39	0.19	0.07	334.65	1	0	0
Missouri	1.14	4.49	108.00	0.96	0.02	0.03	82.31	1	1	1
Nebraska	1.07	5.06	74.20	0.84	0.09	0.03	71.40	0	1	0
New Jersey	0.65	2.74	86.30	0.16	0.01	0.17	494.60	0	1	0
New York	1.35	2.72	124.20	2.08	0.01	0.24	NA	1	1	0
North Carolina	0.34	3.53	54.70	0.64	0.03	0.04	73.57	1	0	1
Ohio	0.49	4.80	122.50	0.87	0.02	0.11	155.69	1	1	0
Oklahoma	0.98	5.71	57.20	0.65	0.04	0.02	75.25	0	1	1
Oregon	0.60	3.66	70.70	1.19	0.15	0.10	81.48	1	0	0
Pennsylvania	0.56	5.02	98.50	1.26	0.03	0.07	173.42	0	1	0
Rhode Island	1.02	5.81	102.40	0.24	0.00	0.08	75.13	1	1	0
South Carolina	0.75	3.29	89.60	0.00	0.00	0.02	49.58	0	0	1

TABLE 4 (Continued)

State	Diabetes	Heart	Cancer	Public TV	Public Radio	Planned Parenthood	AIDS	Moral	Indiv	Trad
Tennessee	0.49	6.01	69.50	0.50	0.03	0.03	442.29	0	0	1
Texas	0.68	5.22	87.30	0.61	0.01	0.03	163.10	0	1	1
Utah	0.64	4.95	83.00	0.80	0.15	0.03	25.46	1	0	0
Virginia	0.76	6.70	114.60	0.49	0.02	0.08	79.62	0	0	1
Washington	1.02	4.12	91.10	1.74	0.05	0.11	65.17	1	1	0
Wisconsin	NA	5.02	90.90	1.06	0.06	0.05	156.37	1	0	0

Diabetes, Heart, Cancer, Public TV and Radio, Planned Parenthood, and AIDS = Contributions per capita (or relative to effective buying income) to the respective campaigns, 1990.

Moral, Indiv, and Trad = Daniel Elazar scoring of states according to moral, individualistic, and traditional orientations (1 = dominant category, 0 = minor presence).

Source: Elazar, Daniel. American Federalism: A View from the States (New York: Thomas Y. Crowell Co., 1972).

NA = not available.

* The District of Columbia is included as a state for purposes of comparison.

TABLE 5
MEASURES OF STATE PUBLIC GENEROSITY

State	Arts Expend	Library Empl	Income Tax	Tax Capacity	Tax Effort	Medicaid/ Recipient	Public Welfare	AFDC/ Family	Teachers' Salaries	School Expend	Educ Index	Income/ Capita	Total Population
Alabama	36.1	1.6	11.9	76	84	1.46	170	114	25,190	3,314	0.919	13,679	4,040,587
Arizona	70.9	3.1	10.7	99	96	2.21	238	268	28,684	4,151	1.008	15,881	3,665,228
California	58.5	4.1	18.8	116	94	1.42	433	590	35,285	4,645	1.059	19,740	29,760,021
Colorado	38.6	3.9	13.4	107	89	2.42	271	318	29,558	4,580	0.998	17,494	3,294,394
Connecticut	67.0	4.8	8.9	143	90	3.93	405	491	37,339	7,876	1.258	24,604	3,287,116
Delaware	158.6	1.2	22.7	124	84	2.73	200	270	31,605	5,858	1.032	19,116	666,168
District of Columbia*	573.5	6.9	1.9	123	154	3.71	994	347	37,504	4,590	0.950	23,436	606,900
Florida	189.6	2.6	1.9	104	82	1.94	197	241	26,648	5,051	0.973	17,694	12,937,926
Georgia	52.4	2.3	16.8	94	89	2.06	261	258	28,038	4,468	0.941	16,188	6,478,216
Hawaii	783.5	5.1	18.6	114	112	1.69	288	506	30,778	4,623	0.950	18,306	1,108,229
Illinois	92.3	5.0	13.1	99	102	1.78	343	309	31,195	4,787	0.974	18,858	11,430,602
Indiana	42.3	6.2	14.5	87	93	3.44	265	263	28,664	4,114	0.929	16,005	5,544,159
Kansas	51.2	2.5	14.8	91	104	1.99	225	339	27,401	4,850	0.917	16,182	2,477,574
Kentucky	63.8	2.1	17.9	81	88	1.67	303	209	24,920	3,793	0.921	13,777	3,685,296
Louisiana	20.0	3.3	6.9	83	90	1.79	251	167	22,470	3,836	0.934	13,041	4,219,973
Maryland	135.7	5.2	26.1	109	108	2.63	336	336	33,700	5,857	1.108	21,020	4,781,468
Massachusetts	209.4	6.4	25.7	129	94	3.67	559	545	31,670	6,172	1.218	22,196	6,016,425
Michigan	137.2	3.5	20.3	95	112	1.64	476	480	34,419	5,049	0.954	17,745	9,295,297
Minnesota	96.9	4.7	19.6	104	112	3.27	497	520	31,500	3,119	0.903	17,746	4,375,099
Missouri	97.0	4.3	16.8	90	86	1.81	224	263	25,981	4,226	0.929	16,431	5,117,073
Nebraska	64.5	3.2	11.4	90	98	2.16	273	323	24,203	3,874	0.929	15,360	1,578,385
New Jersey	252.0	4.6	14.2	124	101	3.22	381	357	32,923	8,439	1.258	23,764	7,730,188
New York	252.0	3.6	24.9	109	152	4.16	707	536	32,923	7,917	1.132	20,540	17,990,455
North Carolina	76.6	2.8	22.6	91	93	2.33	219	243	25,650	4,373	0.936	15,221	6,628,637
Ohio	111.9	5.5	19.6	91	97	2.11	413	297	29,152	5,195	0.958	16,499	10,847,115
Oklahoma	98.4	2.2	11.3	89	89	2.38	291	281	22,000	3,439	0.925	14,151	3,145,585
Oregon	50.2	2.7	17.1	91	99	1.75	235	349	29,500	5,047	0.942	15,785	2,842,321
Pennsylvania	108.2	1.7	17.4	94	97	2.07	382	352	30,720	6,111	1.013	17,422	11,881,643
Rhode Island	138.8	3.1	15.3	99	104	3.39	497	455	34,233	6,425	1.068	18,061	1,003,464

TABLE 5 (Continued)

State	Arts Expend	Library Empl	Income Tax	Tax Capacity	Tax Effort	Medicaid/ Recipient	Public Welfare	AFDC/ Family	Teachers' Salaries	School Expend	Educ Index	Income/ Capita	Total Population
South Carolina	100.0	2.2	16.4	79	96	1.73	188	189	25,060	3,731	0.926	13,616	3,486,703
Tennessee	81.5	1.9	3.8	84	83	1.86	302	158	25,619	3,518	0.930	14,765	4,877,185
Texas	19.5	2.6	0.0	96	88	1.83	180	169	26,513	4,056	0.941	15,483	16,986,510
Utah	154.2	3.3	15.8	78	106	2.15	224	344	23,023	2,720	0.929	13,027	1,722,850
Virginia	88.5	4.5	19.4	104	91	2.32	202	258	29,056	5,149	0.971	18,970	6,187,358
Washington	48.4	5.4	0.0	98	102	2.11	316	444	29,176	4,590	0.970	17,640	4,866,692
Wisconsin	46.8	4.4	19.0	90	119	2.44	476	472	31,046	5,703	0.954	16,759	4,891,769
Mean	129.6	3.7	15.2	99.3	99.4	2.4	339.5	335.0	29,259.6	4,867.9	1.0	17,395	229,454,611

Arts Expend = Per capita state expenditures for the arts, 1990.
Library Empl = State and local library employment per 10,000 state population, 1987.
Income Tax = Percentage of state and local revenue from income and corporation taxes.
Tax Capacity = Amount of revenue raised with use of national average tax rates, 1988.
Tax Effort = Ratio of actual state tax collection to its tax capacity, 1988.
Medicaid/Recipient = Medicaid benefits per recipient, 1988.
Public Welfare = State and local public welfare employment per 10,000 state population.
AFDC/Family = Average monthly payment per AFDC family, 1988.
Teachers' Salaries = Average teachers' salaries, 1988.
School Expend = Average expenditures per pupil, 1989.
Educ Index = Rating of educational quality, educational testing service, 1989.
Income/Capita = Income per capita, 1989.
Total Population = State population, 1990.

*The District of Columbia is included as a state for purposes of comparison.

TABLE 6

CORRELATION OF HUMAN SERVICE AND AMENITIES INDICES
FOR METROPOLITAN AREAS AND THEIR RESPECTIVE STATES

	MAI	MHSI	SAI	SHSI
Metro Amenity Index (MAI)	*	0.00	0.21	0.20
Metro Human Service Index (MHSI)		*	0.21	0.02
State Amenity Index (SAI)			*	0.81
State Human Service Index (SHSI)				*

Where indices represent the composite "z" scores for the measures used in Tables 5, 7, and 8.

TABLE 7

COMPARATIVE RESOURCES OF METROPOLITAN AREAS

Metropolitan Area	Wealth 1990	Population 1990	Population % 1980–90	Employment 1989	Income PC1989	Income % 1980–90	Jobs % 1980–90	Fortune 500
Akron	93.90	657,575	0	254,953	16,499	334	262	4
Albany	102.01	874,304	5	361,876	20,540	639	446	1
Allentown	99.34	686,688	8	132,764	17,422	502	328	2
Anaheim–Santa Ana	137.13	2,410,556	25	1,327,624	19,740	632	683	5
Atlanta	113.42	2,833,511	33	1,271,474	16,188	537	659	6
Austin	96.19	781,572	46	307,568	15,483	705	895	1
Baltimore	110.84	2,382,172	8	1,127,504	21,020	546	452	2
Bergen–Passaic	151.75	1,278,440	–1	464,811	23,764	651	482	7
Birmingham	91.76	907,810	3	397,177	13,679	386	388	1
Boston	127.90	2,870,669	3	1,289,831	22,196	756	532	11
Buffalo	98.97	968,532	–5	422,088	20,540	498	307	1
Charlotte	98.97	1,162,093	20	377,421	15,221	473	506	1
Chicago	117.22	6,069,974	0	3,066,447	18,858	377	431	36
Cincinnati	101.98	1,452,645	4	685,421	16,499	415	420	4
Cleveland	107.18	1,831,122	–4	756,988	16,499	386	426	13
Columbus	96.72	1,377,419	11	558,395	16,499	420	429	1
Dallas	114.44	2,553,362	30	1,051,644	15,483	746	798	14
Dayton	94.74	951,270	1	442,123	16,499	325	276	4
Denver	111.82	1,622,980	14	741,595	17,494	745	700	5
Detroit	107.80	4,382,299	–2	1,905,201	17,745	157	157	8
Fort Lauderdale	126.00	1,255,488	23	609,777	17,694	693	749	0
Fort Worth	100.19	1,332,053	37	581,197	15,483	621	710	0
Fresno	85.71	667,490	30	278,131	19,740	471	648	0
Gary	87.86	604,526	–6	209,835	16,005	230	165	0
Grand Rapids	101.42	688,399	14	278,978	17,745	306	422	1
Greensboro/Winston–Salem	101.60	942,091	11	358,406	15,221	411	429	3
Greenville–Spartanburg	89.36	640,861	12	285,191	13,616	449	406	2
Harrisburg	96.57	587,986	6	195,173	17,422	495	396	3

TABLE 7 (Continued)

Metropolitan Area	Wealth 1990	Population 1990	Population % 1980–90	Employment 1989	Income PC1989	Income % 1980–90	Jobs % 1980–90	Fortune 500
Hartford	128.45	767,841	7	350,494	24,604	721	531	4
Honolulu	104.43	836,231	10	371,621	18,306	434	707	0
Houston	101.48	3,301,937	21	1,513,300	15,483	677	767	18
Indianapolis	104.18	1,249,822	7	610,392	16,005	311	346	2
Jacksonville	93.05	906,727	26	405,319	17,694	543	580	1
Jersey City	99.10	553,099	-1	231,164	23,764	485	304	1
Kansas City					16,182	434	530	0
Kansas City MO	105.85	1,566,280	9	717,565	16,431	386	307	2
Knoxville	88.41	604,816	7	154,680	14,765	510	594	0
Los Angeles	110.72	8,863,164	19	4,301,334	19,740	535	454	12
Louisville	97.92	952,662	0	448,598	13,777	384	462	1
Memphis	93.26	981,747	7	460,885	14,765	404	434	1
Miami	99.83	1,937,094	19	893,976	17,694	526	571	2
Middlesex–Somerset	146.99	1,019,835	15	295,969	23,764	662	550	4
Milwaukee	105.13	1,432,149	3	718,234	16,759	452	285	6
Minneapolis	114.18	2,464,124	15	1,199,564	17,746	501	473	15
Monmouth–Ocean	133.50	986,327	16	291,989	23,764	665	615	2
Nashville	99.93	985,026	16	421,475	14,765	474	639	0
Nassau–Suffolk	142.27	2,609,212	0	1,392,740	20,540	811	654	2
New Haven	119.06	530,180	6	256,996	24,604	613	424	2
New Orleans	88.99	1,238,816	-1	515,827	13,041	729	525	4
New York City	117.86	8,546,846	3	3,605,969	20,540	598	458	45
Newark	136.81	1,824,321	-3	354,417	23,764	682	482	6
Norfolk	90.77	1,396,107	20	576,106	18,970	655	537	0
Oakland	124.04	2,082,914	18	1,898,631	19,740	557	478	2
Oklahoma City	88.9	958,839	11	322,003	14,151	883	761	1
Omaha	98.42	618,262	6	292,988	15,360	468	486	3
Orlando	97.04	1,072,748	53	558,639	17,694	720	936	0
Oxnard–Ventura	118.08	669,016	26	340,470	19,740	532	625	1

TABLE 7 (Continued)

Metropolitan Area	Wealth 1990	Population 1990	Population % 1980–90	Employment 1989	Income PC1989	Income % 1980–90	Jobs % 1980–90	Fortune 500
Philadelphia	109.86	4,856,881	3	1,865,839	17,422	549	416	11
Phoenix	102.74	2,122,101	41	737,425	15,881	561	760	1
Pittsburgh	98.97	2,056,705	-7	901,305	17,422	553	322	12
Portland	101.19	1,239,842	12	704,756	15,785	279	390	5
Providence	99.70	654,854	6	546,569	18,061	533	404	3
Raleigh	105.58	735,480	31	403,599	15,221	578	680	0
Richmond	111.72	865,640	14	422,875	18,970	552	480	6
Riverside	86.82	2,588,793	66	161,854	19,740	381	506	1
Rochester	106.59	1,002,410	3	463,812	20,540	677	596	2
Sacramento	98.69	1,481,102	35	653,692	19,740	341	592	0
Salt Lake City	81.49	1,072,227	18	392,047	13,027	377	542	1
San Antonio	84.37	1,302,099	21	510,337	15,483	736	693	3
San Diego	104.63	2,498,016	34	1,102,251	19,740	543	604	1
San Francisco	154.06	1,603,678	8	1,898,631	19,740	640	538	6
San Jose	134.27	1,497,577	16	812,003	19,740	849	801	15
Scranton	86.97	734,175	1	237,838	17,422	516	341	0
Seattle	114.98	1,972,961	23	1,011,559	17,640	427	572	3
Springfield	101.07	529,519	4	174,986	22,196	560	381	1
St. Louis	109.09	2,444,099	3	996,271	16,431	498	401	8
Syracuse	95.13	659,864	3	226,822	20,540	673	627	2
Tampa	102.28	2,067,959	28	818,341	17,694	728	809	2
Toledo	95.74	614,128	0	302,719	16,499	299	296	4
Tucson	88.50	666,880	25	219,023	15,881	612	697	1
Tulsa	94.87	708,954	8	244,633	14,151	691	668	2
West Palm Beach	143.59	863,518	50	317,400	17,694	740	935	1
Washington	133.34	3,923,574	21	2,070,976	23,436	617	552	9
Wilmington	110.74	578,587	11	280,827	19,116	554	552	4
Youngstown	87.49	492,619	-7	214,208	16,499	226	128	0
Mean	105.36	137,564,271	12	728,630	17,961	536	521	4.4

TABLE 7 (Continued)

Wealth = Woods and Poole index of wages, rents, and dividends.
Pop 1990 = MSA population, U.S. Census.
Pop % 1980–90 = Percent change in MSA population 1980–90.
Emp 1989 = Employment in MSA, 1989.
Income PC 1989 = Income per capita in MSA, 1989.
Income % 1980–90 = Relative index of income growth, 1980–90, Woods and Poole.
Jobs % 1980–90 = Relative index of job growth, 1980–90, Woods and Poole
Fortune 500 = Number of Fortune 500 firms with headquarters in MSA.

TABLE 8

MEASURES OF STATE RESOURCES AND DISTRESS

State	Tax Capacity	Tax Effort	Income PC 1989	Population 1990	Pop % 80–90	Income PC %79–89	Medicaid Pop 1981	Medicaid Pop 1989	Medicaid Pop 1981–89	Local Fisc Disparity
Alabama	76	84	13,679	4,040,587	3.8	93.6	331	305	-8	94
Arizona	99	96	15,881	3,665,228	34.9	91.0	0	0	NA	116
California	116	94	19,740	29,760,021	25.7	87.5	3,617	3,674	2	80
Colorado	107	89	17,494	3,294,394	14.0	85.1	146	180	24	113
Connecticut	143	90	24,604	3,287,116	5.8	129.4	222	221	-1	87
Delaware	124	84	19,116	666,168	12.1	108.2	50	37	-27	NA
District of Columbia*	123	154	23,436	606,900	-4.9	107.4	121	97	-20	NA
Florida	104	82	17,694	12,937,926	32.8	102.9	539	768	42	146
Georgia	94	89	16,188	6,478,216	18.6	112.7	443	537	21	102
Hawaii	114	112	18,306	1,108,229	14.8	92.6	105	91	-13	NA
Illinois	99	102	18,858	11,430,602	0.0	86.9	1,111	1,043	-6	96
Indiana	87	93	16,005	5,544,159	1.0	84.1	222	301	35	67
Kansas	91	104	16,182	2,477,574	4.8	74.2	149	170	14	70
Kentucky	81	88	13,777	3,685,296	0.7	86.6	413	413	0	159
Louisiana	83	90	13,041	4,219,973	0.3	70.1	410	432	5	132
Maryland	109	108	21,020	4,781,468	13.4	117.3	328	320	-2	93
Massachusetts	129	94	22,196	6,016,425	4.9	135.0	747	556	-26	102
Michigan	95	112	17,745	9,295,297	0.4	85.3	962	1,104	15	95
Minnesota	104	112	17,746	4,375,099	7.3	92.3	324	336	4	86
Missouri	90	86	16,431	5,117,073	4.1	90.7	361	379	5	120
Nebraska	90	98	15,360	1,578,385	0.5	73.5	76	105	37	81
New Jersey	124	101	23,764	7,730,188	5.0	131.2	661	533	-19	123
New York	109	152	20,540	17,990,455	2.5	113.5	2,241	2,212	-1	87
North Carolina	91	93	15,221	6,628,637	12.7	108.6	382	411	7	96
Ohio	91	97	16,499	10,847,115	0.5	84.2	857	1,117	30	85
Oklahoma	89	89	14,151	3,145,585	4.0	69.0	278	245	-12	124
Oregon	91	99	15,785	2,842,321	7.9	72.1	171	189	11	61
Pennsylvania	94	97	17,422	11,881,643	0.1	93.7	1,090	1,086	0	76
Rhode Island	99	104	18,061	1,003,464	6.0	113.9	127	98	-23	72

TABLE 8 (Continued)

State	Tax Capacity	Tax Effort	Income PC 1989	Population 1990	Pop % 80–90	Income PC %79–89	Medicaid Pop 1981	Medicaid Pop 1989	Medicaid Pop 1981–89	Local Fisc Disparity
South Carolina	79	96	13,616	3,486,703	11.7	97.6	366	263	-28	106
Tennessee	84	83	14,765	4,877,185	6.2	99.8	364	479	32	127
Texas	96	88	15,483	16,986,510	19.4	75.3	706	1,062	50	128
Utah	78	106	13,027	1,722,850	17.9	75.9	68	86	26	113
Virginia	104	91	18,970	6,187,358	15.7	117.8	331	326	-1	111
Washington	98	102	17,640	4,866,692	17.8	79.3	331	403	22	80
Wisconsin	90	119	16,759	4,891,769	3.9	84.7	445	403	-9	88
Mean	99.3	99.4	17,395	229,454,611	9.1	95.1	19,095	19,982	5	100

Tax Capacity = Advisory Commission on Intergovernmental Relations (ACIR) index of revenues states would raise using national average tax rates, 1988.

Tax Effort = ACIR index of state's tax collections relative to its tax capacity, 1988.

Income PC 1989 = Per capita income of state's residents, 1989.

Population 1990 = State population, 1990.

Pop % 80–90 = Percentage change in population, 1980–90.

Income PC %79–89 = Percentage change in per capital income, 1979–89.

Medicaid Pop = Number of state residents on Medicaid, 1981 and 1989.

Local Fisc Disparity = Ranking of states by extent of local fiscal disparities, assuming no state and federal general fiscal assistance, 1985.

Source: General Accounting Office.

*The District of Columbia is included as a state for purposes of comparison.

TABLE 9

COMPARATIVE DISTRESS MEASURES IN METROPOLITAN AREAS

Metropolitan Area	Metro Pop % 1980–90	CC Pop % 1980–90	Unemp % 1990	Unemp % 1989	Metro Pov % 1979	CC Pov % 1979	Metro Pov % 1989	CC Pov % 1989	LBW % 1988	Trans-fers % 1989	FEM-HHD % 1990	IDR 1987	Teen-Born 1987
Akron	0	-5	5.3	5.5	9	15	12	21	6.6	16.0	11.8	10.0	11.4
Albany	5	-2	4.4	3.7	10	18	9	18	6.0	17.3	10.7	8.1	9.2
Allentown	8	1	5.7	3.9	7	12	7	13	5.7	14.2	9.3	8.5	9.0
Anaheim–Santa Ana	25	32	4.0	3.0	7	8	8	11	5.0	8.7	9.7	7.5	8.3
Atlanta	33	-4	5.8	4.9	13	28	10	27	7.9	8.9	13.0	11.7	13.1
Austin	46	25	4.7	5.6	14	16	15	18	5.9	11.4	10.2	7.3	12.0
Baltimore	8	-6	6.8	4.5	12	23	10	22	8.5	12.0	14.6	12.6	13.5
Bergen–Passaic	-1	2	5.0	2.6	7	25	6	19	6.4	9.5	11.2	7.7	7.0
Birmingham	3	-8	5.0	5.9	15	22	15	25	8.5	15.0	13.9	11.9	14.9
Boston	3	3	5.8	3.2	9	20	8	19	6.0	12.8	12.1	7.2	7.2
Buffalo	-5	-8	5.3	5.7	11	21	12	26	7.1	18.5	13.3	10.1	10.0
Charlotte	20	17	4.3	3.0	11	12	10	11	8.8	10.7	12.0	12.8	16.2
Chicago	0	-7	5.6	5.5	12	20	12	22	8.3	12.3	14.1	13.0	12.5
Cincinnati	4	-6	3.8	4.6	10	20	12	24	6.6	14.6	12.6	9.1	13.5
Cleveland	-4	-12	4.7	4.9	10	22	12	29	7.9	16.2	13.6	10.7	11.8
Columbus	11	11	4.3	4.5	11	17	12	17	7.0	14.7	11.6	8.8	12.4
Dallas	30	15	5.4	5.6	10	14	12	18	7.3	8.2	11.4	9.3	14.2
Dayton	1	-5	5.2	5.0	10	21	12	27	7.0	17.1	12.0	8.5	13.7
Denver	14	-5	4.3	5.9	8	14	10	17	8.4	11.0	10.5	10.4	10.2
Detroit	-2	-13	7.1	7.9	10	22	13	32	8.3	14.3	15.1	11.9	12.0
Fort Lauderdale	23	2	5.2	4.7	9	14	10	17	8.1	13.8	10.0	10.6	10.1
Fort Worth	37	30	5.7	5.8	9	14	11	17	6.6	10.2	10.5	9.7	13.9
Fresno	30	41	12.0	10.2	15	16	21	24	6.5	18.2	13.9	8.6	14.5
Gary	-6	-18	5.0	5.6	10	20	12	29	8.1	15.2	14.3	10.1	13.5
Grand Rapids	14	5	5.9	5.2	8	14	8	16	5.6	11.5	10.3	10.1	10.1
Greensboro/Winston–Salem	11	4	4.4	3.3	11	13	10	12	8.4	11.1	11.8	11.4	14.6
Greenville–Spartanburg	12	0	4.5	3.1	12	20	11	18	8.5	12.5	12.0	13.2	16.4
Harrisburg	6	-2	4.4	3.6	8	23	8	27	6.1	16.1	9.6	10.4	11.1

TABLE 9 (Continued)

Metropolitan Area	Metro Pop % 1980–90	CC Pop % 1980–90	Unemp % 1990	Unemp % 1989	Metro Pov % 1979	CC Pov % 1979	Metro Pov % 1989	CC Pov % 1989	LBW % 1988	Trans-fers % 1989	FEM-HHD % 1990	IDR 1987	Teen-Born 1987
Hartford	7	4	4.2	3.0	8	25	8	28	6.8	11.1	11.6	9.5	8.7
Honolulu	10	0	2.1	2.8	10	10	7	8	6.9	12.6	10.5	9.6	9.4
Houston	21	1	5.4	6.0	10	13	15	21	7.3	8.9	12.3	9.4	12.9
Indianapolis	7	4	4.4	3.9	9	12	10	13	7.3	11.9	11.7	12.5	14.1
Jacksonville	26	17	5.4	5.6	15	16	12	13	7.6	14.4	12.6	10.9	14.3
Jersey City	-1	-2	8.1	6.2	17	21	15	19	8.8	16.5	16.5	10.0	11.5
Kansas City	9	1	4.8	6.8	9	13	10	15	6.8	12.0	11.3	11.4	12.5
Kansas City MO	9	1	4.8	5.0	9	13	10	15	6.8	12.0	11.3	11.4	12.5
Knoxville	7	-5	5.3	4.8	15	20	14	21	7.0	15.5	10.8	10.5	14.1
Los Angeles	19	18	6.2	4.6	13	16	15	19	6.3	12.6	13.1	9.8	11.5
Louisville	0	-9	4.8	5.8	11	19	13	23	7.1	14.3	13.5	8.5	14.8
Memphis	7	-5	5.0	5.0	20	22	18	23	10.0	15.0	17.9	15.3	17.8
Miami	19	9	6.0	6.0	15	25	18	31	8.2	14.4	14.9	10.3	11.0
Middlesex–Somerset	15	4	4.3	2.4	6	24	4	22	5.6	7.9	9.2	7.9	5.1
Milwaukee	3	0	3.6	3.6	8	14	12	22	6.8	14.5	13.0	9.5	12.7
Minneapolis	15	1	4.1	3.6	7	14	8	19	5.3	11.0	9.7	8.7	7.1
Monmouth–Ocean	16	16	5.6	3.2	8	8	5	5	5.9	12.3	9.3	8.2	6.6
Nashville	16	9	4.2	4.2	12	13	11	13	7.8	11.7	12.2	9.9	13.9
Nassau–Suffolk	0	0	4.3	3.8	6	6	4	4	6.0	11.3	10.3	9.0	4.9
New Haven	6	3	4.5	3.3	10	23	8	21	7.4	12.9	12.5	9.3	9.4
New Orleans	-1	-11	5.4	9.1	17	26	21	32	9.4	15.9	17.5	12.3	15.0
New York City	3	4	5.9	5.0	18	20	17	19	9.3	17.3	17.1	12.1	10.0
Newark	-3	-12	5.7	4.9	11	33	9	26	8.3	11.2	14.1	10.4	10.4
Norfolk	20	17	5.0	4.6	14	21	11	19	7.1	14.6	13.1	19.3	12.9
Oakland	18	8	4.6	4.0	10	19	9	19	6.9	12.3	12.1	8.2	8.5
Oklahoma City	11	10	6.2	5.1	11	12	14	16	7.0	15.8	11.4	10.8	14.2
Omaha	6	-3	2.3	3.5	9	11	10	13	6.2	13.2	11.4	9.3	10.0
Orlando	53	28	5.2	4.9	12	18	10	16	7.3	12.2	11.0	8.8	13.4
Oxnard–Ventura	26	24	6.9	5.3	8	12	7	13	4.9	10.9	9.8	7.4	8.8

TABLE 9 (Continued)

Metropolitan Area	Metro Pop % 1980–90	CC Pop % 1980–90	Unemp % 1990	Unemp % 1989	Metro Pov % 1979	CC Pov % 1979	Metro Pov % 1989	CC Pov % 1989	LBW % 1988	Trans-fers % 1989	FEM-HHD % 1990	IDR 1987	Teen-Born 1987
Philadelphia	3	-6	4.8	3.9	12	21	10	20	8.0	14.9	13.7	11.7	11.3
Phoenix	41	34	4.4	4.8	11	11	12	14	6.2	13.0	10.2	10.0	13.2
Portland	12	1	4.3	4.4	9	13	10	15	5.8	13.1	9.7	10.4	9.5
Providence	6	1	6.1	3.4	10	20	10	23	6.1	16.7	11.9	8.5	10.0
Raleigh	31	26	2.9	2.5	12	12	10	12	6.9	9.9	11.2	13.7	10.4
Richmond	14	-7	4.3	3.4	11	19	10	21	7.9	11.7	13.6	11.5	11.3
Riverside	66	33	8.1	7.0	11	11	12	12	6.5	12.2	11.0	10.5	12.8
Rochester	3	-4	4.3	4.0	9	18	10	24	5.8	14.0	11.7	8.8	9.9
Sacramento	35	36	6.2	5.2	11	15	12	17	6.2	17.5	11.8	9.9	11.1
Salt Lake City	18	-2	3.5	4.2	8	14	9	16	6.2	13.7	10.0	9.1	9.9
San Antonio	21	15	7.1	7.6	18	21	19	23	6.4	17.9	14.0	8.6	16.5
San Diego	34	29	5.4	4.1	11	12	11	13	5.8	14.4	10.8	9.4	9.7
San Francisco	8	7	3.7	4.0	10	14	9	13	5.8	10.1	9.7	6.7	6.1
San Jose	16	21	4.8	3.9	7	8	8	9	5.4	8.6	10.3	8.5	7.7
Scranton	1	-8	7.1	5.6	10	13	11	15	5.8	22.0	11.0	8.6	9.5
Seattle	23	8	3.9	4.5	8	11	8	12	5.3	11.5	9.0	9.6	7.4
Springfield	4	2	7.0	3.8	11	18	12	20	6.7	18.4	14.1	7.5	11.9
St Louis	3	-9	6.0	5.3	10	22	11	25	7.3	13.0	12.6	9.9	12.7
Syracuse	3	-4	5.0	4.0	10	18	10	23	6.7	15.5	11.3	12.3	10.9
Tampa	28	3	4.9	4.7	12	19	11	19	7.7	17.6	9.9	9.0	13.7
Toledo	0	-5	8.1	5.8	11	14	14	19	7.3	17.0	12.5	8.3	14.3
Tucson	25	16	4.1	5.0	13	15	17	20	6.0	17.4	10.9	7.8	12.6
Tulsa	8	2	5.4	6.2	10	10	13	15	6.5	13.1	10.4	8.8	14.0
West Palm Beach	50	20	5.4	5.6	10	16	9	16	7.9	12.3	8.6	13.4	11.8
Washington	21	0	4.0	2.8	8	19	6	17	8.1	11.1	12.0	10.8	8.5
Wilmington	11	2	6.0	3.2	11	25	8	18	7.2	11.3	11.9	10.6	12.9
Youngstown	-7	-15	7.1	6.8	10	18	14	29	7.3	20.7	12.8	10.7	12.6
Mean	12	5	5.2	4.7	11	17	11	19	7.0	13.6	11.9	10.1	11.5

TABLE 9 (Continued)

Metro Pop %1980-90 = Percentage change in MSA population, 1980–90.
CC Pop %1980–90 = Percentage change in MSA's center city population, 1980–90.
Unemp % = Percentage MSA unemployment, 1989 and 1990.
Metro Pov & CC Pov = Poverty percentage in MSA and center city, 1979 and 1989.
LBW % = Percentage of low birth weight babies in MSA, 1988.
Transfers = Percentage MSA income from transfer programs, 1989.
FemHHD = Percentage of MSA households headed by females, 1990.
IDR = Infant death rate, 1987.
Teenborn = Percentage of MSA births to teenage mothers, 1987.

TABLE 10
RELATING GENEROSITY TO AFFLUENCE AND DISTRESS, 1990
REGRESSION ANALYSES — BETA COEFFICIENTS/PROBABILITIES

	UW Donations per Employee	Nonprofit Expend per Capita	Human Service Share
Population	-0.39 0.93	-0.17 0.60	-0.63 0.99
Wealth	-0.25 0.95	0.06 0.37	0.26 0.97
Fortune 500	0.44 0.96	0.34 0.91	0.52 0.99
Unemployment	-0.38 0.99	-0.08 0.52	0.15 0.79
ACU Index	-0.09 0.53	-0.37 0.99	0.19 0.87
Nonprofit expend per capita	0.00 0.02		-0.27 0.97
Human service share	0.02 0.16	-0.24 0.97	
UW donations per employee		0.00 0.02	0.02 0.16
R-squared	0.22	0.34	0.27

Source: Noted in the text.

Notes

Chapter 1

1. Paul E. Peterson and Mark C. Rom, *Welfare Magnets: A New Case for a National Standard* (Washington, D.C.: The Brookings Institution, 1990).

Chapter 2

1. D. Collard, *Altruism and Economy* (Oxford: Robertson, 1978); Julian Wolpert, "Key Indicators of Generosity in Communities," in Virginia A. Hodgkinson and Richard W. Lyman, eds., *The Future of the Nonprofit Sector* (San Francisco: Jossey-Bass, 1989).

2. T. Ball, "The Incoherence of Intergenerational Justice," *Inquiry* 28, no. 3 (1986): 321–37.

3. Stanley N. Katz, "Influences on Public Policies in the United States," in W. McNeil Lowry ed., *The Arts and Public Policy in the United States* (Englewood Cliffs, N.J.: Prentice Hall, 1984).

Chapter 3

1. Thomas R. Swartz and John E. Peck, *The Changing Face of Fiscal Federalism* (Armonk, N.Y.: M. E. Sharpe, Inc., 1990); Richard P. Nathan et al., *Reagan and the States* (Princeton, N.J.: Princeton University Press, 1987); Harvey S. Rosen ed., *Fiscal Federalism: Quantitative Studies* (Chicago: University of Chicago Press, 1988); Lester M. Salamon and Alan J. Abramson, *The Federal Budget and the Nonprofit Sector: FY 1992* (Washington, D.C.: Institute for Policy Studies, Johns Hopkins University, 1991); and Burton A. Weisbrod, *The Nonprofit Economy* (Cambridge, Mass.: Harvard University Press, 1988).

2. Wallace E. Oates, "Decentralization of the Public Sector: An Overview," in R. Bennett, ed., *Decentralization, Local Governments, and Markets* (Oxford: Oxford University Press, 1990), pp. 43–58.

3. Peterson and Rom, *Welfare Magnets*.

4. Weisbrod, *The Nonprofit Economy*.

5. Peter D. Hall, "A Historical Overview of the Private Nonprofit Sector," in W. W. Powell, ed., *The Nonprofit Sector: A Research Handbook* (New Haven: Yale University Press, 1987); Jennifer R. Wolch, *The Shadow State: Government and Voluntary Sector in Transition* (New York: The Foundation Center, 1990); and Lester M. Salamon and Alan J. Abramson, "The Nonprofit Sector," in John L. Palmer and Isabel V. Sawhill, eds., *The Reagan Experiment* (Washington, D.C.: The Urban Institute, 1982).

6. Lester M. Salamon, "Partners in Public Service: The Scope and Theory of Government–Nonprofit Relations," in W. W. Powell, ed., *The Nonprofit Sector.*

7. Hall, "A Historical Overview of the Private Nonprofit Sector."

8. Richard Musgrave, "Leviathan Cometh—or Does He?" in Helen Ladd and T. Nicolaus Tideman, eds., *Tax and Expenditure Limitations* (Washington, D.C.: The Urban Institute, 1981); and Wallace E. Oates, *Studies in Fiscal Federalism* (Hants, England: Edward Elgar, 1991).

9. Geoffrey Brennan and James Buchanan, *The Power to Tax: Analytical Foundations of a Fiscal Constitution* (Cambridge: Cambridge University Press, 1980).

10. General Accounting Office, *Communities in Fiscal Distress: State Grant Targeting Provides Limited Help*, GAO HRD–90–69, Washington, D.C., April 1990.

11. Nathan et al., *Reagan and the States.*

Chapter 4

1. Virginia Hodgkinson et al., *Nonprofit Almanac: Dimensions of the Independent Sector, 1992–93* (San Francisco: Jossey-Bass, 1992).

2. AAFRC Trust for Philanthropy, *'92 Giving USA* (New York: American Association of Fund-Raising Counsel, 1992).

3. Salamon and Abramson, *The Federal Budget and the Nonprofit Sector.*

4. Charles Tiebout,"A Pure Theory of Local Expenditures," *Journal of Political Economy*, 64 (October 1956): 416–24.

Chapter 5

1. Eleanor L. Brilliant, *The United Way: Dilemmas of Organized Charity* (New York: Columbia University Press, 1990).

2. The beta coefficients in the regression analysis are virtually the same as those for the changes in United Way contributions.

3. Lester M. Salamon, "The Charitable Behavior of the Charitable Sector: The Case of Social Services," in Charles T. Clotfelter, ed., *Who Benefits from the Nonprofit Sector?* (Chicago: University of Chicago Press, 1992).

4. Ibid.

5. Kirsten A. Gronbjerg et al., "Nonprofit Human Service Facilities in Illinois: Structure, Adequacy, and Management," report prepared for the Illinois Facilities Fund, Chicago, 1992; Salamon, "The Charitable Behavior of the Charitable Sector."

6. Salamon, "The Charitable Behavior of the Charitable Sector."

Chapter 6

1. Peterson and Rom, *Welfare Magnets.*

2. General Accounting Office, *Communities in Fiscal Distress.*

Index

About the Author

Julian Wolpert is the Henry G. Bryant Professor of Geography, Public Affairs and Urban Planning at the Woodrow Wilson School of Public and International Affairs, Princeton University, and is director of the Program in Urban and Regional Planning. Formerly a professor of regional science and geography at the University of Pennsylvania, Dr. Wolpert has been a Guggenheim Foundation Fellow, a Woodrow Wilson Internatinoal Center for Scholars Fellow, and a Bellagio Study Center Fellow, Rockefeller Foundation. Dr. Wolpert is a member of the National Academy of Sciences, a Fellow of the American Association for the Advancement of Science, and the author of numerous articles on philanthropy, regional economies, and the nonprofit sector.